VOID
Library of
Davidson College

TWO ISSUES IN PUBLIC-KEY CRYPTOGRAPHY

ACM Distinguished Dissertations

1982

Abstraction Mechanisms and Language Design
by Paul N. Hilfinger

Formal Specification of Interactive Graphics Programming Language
by William R. Mallgren

Algorithmic Program Debugging
by Ehud Y. Shapiro

1983

The Measurement of Visual Motion
by Ellen Catherine Hildreth

Synthesis of Digital Designs from Recursion Equations
by Steven D. Johnson

1984

Analytic Methods in the Analysis and Design of Number-Theoretic Algorithms
by Eric Bach

Model-Based Image Matching Using Location
by Henry S. Baird

A Geometric Investigation of Reach
by James U. Korein

1985

Two Issues in Public-Key Cryptography
by Ben-Zion Chor

The Connection Machine
by W. Daniel Hillis

TWO ISSUES IN PUBLIC-KEY CRYPTOGRAPHY
RSA BIT SECURITY
AND
A NEW KNAPSACK TYPE SYSTEM

Ben-Zion Chor

The MIT Press
Cambridge, Massachusetts
London, England

© 1986 by The Massachusetts Institute of Technology

All rights reserved. No part of this book may be reproduced in any form by any electronic or mechanical means (including photocopying, recording, or information storage and retrieval) without permission in writing from the publisher.

This dissertation was submitted in June 1985 to the Department of Electrical Engineering and Computer Science, the Massachusetts Institute of Technology, in partial fulfillment of the degree of Doctor of Philosophy.

Printed and bound in the United States of America.

Library of Congress Cataloging-in-Publication Data

Chor, Ben-Zion.
  Two issues in public-key cryptography.

  (ACM distinguished dissertations; 1985)
  Originally presented as the author's thesis (doctoral)—MIT, 1985.
  Bibliography: p.
  1. Telecommunication—Security measures. 2. Cryptography. I. Title. II. Series.
TK5102.5.C478   1986   384′.028′9   85-24072
ISBN 0-262-03121-3

To my parents
Moshe and Nehama

CONTENTS

1. Introduction — 1

Part I. RSA Bit Security

2. Background — 7
  2.1 The RSA Cryptosystem — 7
  2.2 Multiplicative and Additive Properties of the RSA — 8
  2.3 Predicate Security — 10
  2.4 Some Predicates and Relations Among Them — 12
3. Very Reliable Oracles — 14
  3.1 Binary Search Inversion — 14
  3.2 Parity Information From Reliable Least Significant Bit Oracle — 16
4. Inverting RSA with a Reliable Parity Subroutine — 19
  4.1 General Plan — 19
  4.2 Brent-Kung GCD — 20
  4.3 GCD Inversion Using a Parity Subroutine — 21
  4.4 Reliable Parity Subroutine from $\frac{1}{4} + \frac{1}{poly(n)}$ Oracle — 23
5. The Least Significant Bit is $\frac{1}{poly(n)}$ Secure — 26
  5.1 Error Doubling and Attempts to Overcome it — 26
  5.2 Schnorr and Alexi Improvement — 27
  5.3 Two Points Based Sampling — 28
  5.4 Probability Analysis — 29
6. Extensions and Applications — 33
  6.1 Simultaneous Security — 33
  6.2 Secure Bits in Rabin's Encryption Function — 35
  6.3 Multi Prime Moduli with Partial Factorization — 38
  6.4 Direct Construction of Pseudo Random Bit Generators — 39
  6.5 Applications to Probabilistic Encryption — 40

Part II. A New Knapsack Type Cryptosystem

7. The New Cryptosystem — 43
  7.1 Background — 43

7.2 Knapsack Type Cryptosystems	44
7.3 Bose-Chowla Theorem	45
7.4 How the Cryptosystem is Constructed and Used	47
7.5 System Performance: Time, Space, and Information Rate	50
7.6 Transforming Unconstrained Bit Strings	51
7.7 Proposed Parameters	52
7.8 Implementation Details	53
8. Possible Attacks	**54**
8.1 Specialized Attacks	54
8.2 Low Density Attacks	58
8.3 Countermeasures against Shortest Vector Attacks	59
8.4 Brute Force Attacks	61
8.5 A Word of Caution	62
Appendices	
1. On Discrete Logarithms and Factorization	63
2. Lagarias–Odlyzko Low Density Attack	64
3. A Specific Public-key	67
References	**72**
Index	**77**

Series Foreword

This book is being published by the MIT Press as an outgrowth of the annual contest for the best doctoral dissertation in computer-related science and engineering. The contest was initiated in 1982 by the ACM in cooperation with MIT Press.

The Distinguished Doctoral Dissertation Series has been created to recognize that some of the theses considered in the final round of selecting a contest winner also deserve publication. In the judgment of the ACM selection committee, this thesis is of such high quality that it deserves special recognition in this series.

Dr. Ben-Zion Chor wrote his thesis on "Two Issues in Public-Key Cryptography, RSA Bit Security and a New Knapsack Type System" at the Massachusetts Institute of Technology. The thesis was supervised by Ronald L. Rivest, Professor of Electrical Engineering and Computer Science. The thesis was submitted to the 1985 competition. The ACM Doctoral Dissertation Award Subcommittee recommended publication of this thesis because it makes two major contributions to the field of cryptography. The first part of the thesis analyzes the security of the well-known "RSA" public-key cryptosystem. Dr. Chor demonstrates that under suitable conditions an adversary has no hope of determining the low-order bits of an RSA plaintext from the RSA ciphertext. This definitive theoretical result has practical importance since it provides assurance that the RSA scheme can be used confidently.

The second part of Dr. Chor's thesis deals with cryptographic design and presents a public-key cryptosystem of the "knapsack" type. While previous knapsack-type proposals have been broken, this proposal seems to resist cryptanalysis effectively and, thus, represents one of the first plausible alternatives to the RSA cryptosystem.

John R. White
Chairman, ACM Doctoral Dissertation Award Subcommittee

Preface

This book is a slightly revised version of my MIT dissertation, written in Spring 1985. The general subject of this thesis is public-key cryptographic systems. In the first part of the thesis, we investigate the question of cryptographic security of bits in the RSA encryption. In the second part of the thesis, a new knapsack type public-key cryptosystem, based on arithmetic in finite fields, is constructed.

In the first part of the thesis, we prove that the following two problems are equivalent (each is probabilistic polynomial-time reducible to the other):

1) Given the RSA encryption of a message, retrieve the message.

2) Given the RSA encryption of a message, guess the least-significant bit of the message with success probability $\frac{1}{2} + \frac{1}{poly(n)}$ (where n is the length of the RSA modulus).

This equivalence implies that an adversary, given the ciphertext, cannot have a non-negligible advantage (over a random coin flip) in guessing the least-significant bit of the plaintext, unless he can break RSA. The results are then extended to Rabin's encryption function, and to simultaneous security of the $\log n$ least-significant bits in both RSA and Rabin's functions. This implies that Rabin/RSA encryption can be *directly* used for pseudo random bit generation, provided that factoring/inverting RSA is hard.

In the second part of the thesis, we introduce a new knapsack type public-key cryptosystem, and give a detailed description on its implementation. The system is based on a novel application of arithmetic in finite fields, following a construction by Bose and Chowla. Appropriately choosing the parameters, we can control the density of the resulting knapsack. In particular, the density can be made high enough to foil "low density" attacks against our system. At the moment, we do not know of any attacks capable of "breaking" this system in a reasonable amount of time.

Most of the material in this thesis appeared in preliminary form in three papers, all of which are the result of joint work: "On the Cryptographic Security of Single RSA Bits", joint work with M. Ben-Or and A. Shamir, in *15th ACM Symp. on Theory of Computation*, April 1983. "A knapsack type public-key cryptosystem based on arithmetic in finite fields", joint work with R. Rivest, in *Advances in Cryptology: Proceedings of Crypto84*. "RSA/Rabin least significant bits are $\frac{1}{2} + \frac{1}{poly(n)}$ secure", joint work with O. Goldreich, in *Advances in Cryptology: Proceedings of Crypto84*. This last paper was later combined with the work of W. Alexi and C.P. Schnorr, and titled "RSA and Rabin functions: Certain parts are as hard as the whole", it will appear in *SIAM Jour. on Computing* (extended abstract in *Proc. of the 25th IEEE Symp. on Foundation of Computer Science*, October 1984).

Acknowledgments

First, I would like to thank my advisor, Ron Rivest, for his guidance and encouragement. Ron introduced me to public-key cryptography, which is the subject of this thesis. He always supplied me with insights and criticism which sometimes took me months to fully appreciate. The second part of this thesis is joint work with Ron.

Many other people have contributed to my research at MIT. Charles Leiserson helped me get on the research track when I was still overwhelmed by this new environment. Mike Sipser taught me about complexity theory, and supplied valuable advice and encouragement throughout my work. Michael Ben-Or and Adi Shamir were very helpful in the first stages of the research on the RSA bits. Chapters 3.2 through 4.4 are joint work with both Michael and Adi. Oded Goldreich was indispensable when the work on the RSA bits reached its highest point. Chapters 5 and 6 are joint work with Oded. In addition to his contributions to this research, Oded also provided me with constant feedback on my ideas, and carefully read and commented on the entire thesis. I found the theory group in MIT to be a very lively environment for conducting research. In particular, I benefited from many discussions with Brian Coan, Shafi Goldwasser, Johan Hastad, Nancy Lynch, Mike Merritt, Silvio Micali, and David Shmoys.

Some of the work on part II of the thesis was done while I visited Bell Laboratories in Summer 1983. I'd like to thank Ernie Brickell, Don Coppersmith, Jeff Lagarias, and Andrew Odlyzko for discussions which clarified many of the issues in designing knapsack-type cryptosystems. Andrew's assistance in a first implementation of the system, and later in testing the low density attack against it, were particularly helpful. I'd also like to thank Scott Warner for his assistance in the final implementation of the system, back at MIT.

My work at MIT was supported in part by the National Science Foundation under grant MCS-8006938, and by an IBM Graduate Fellowship.

I am grateful to Oded for his friendship, and to Ron and Shlomit Pinter for their help during my first steps at MIT. Finally, many thanks to Metsada.

CHAPTER 1

INTRODUCTION

The general subject of this thesis is public-key cryptographic systems. The first part of this thesis deals with the analysis of the best known public-key cryptosystems, the RSA. The second part of the thesis deals with the design of a new public-key cryptosystem. In both parts, the corresponding questions are examined from computational complexity point of view.

Cryptography, as a mean for sending secret information over insecure communication channels, is thousands of years old. In conventional cryptosystems, the sender and the receiver possess a joint secret key. The sender uses this key to encrypt the plaintext he sends, while the receiver uses the same key in order to decrypt the ciphertext he gets. Suppose the messages sent are uniformly distributed random strings and the encryption is a permutation of these strings. In such an idealized cryptosystem it is impossible for an eavesdropper to infer any information about the identity of the messages or the key by just observing ciphertexts, no matter how much computing power he possesses. However, the situation changes greatly if the message space has a different distribution than the uniform one. Shanon [47] analyzed this problem quantitatively, introducing the tools of information theory. He showed that every additional ciphertext narrows down the key space, in the sense that certain keys become more and more likely. Ciphertext of sufficient length will determine the key uniquely (with high probability). Given long enough ciphertext, the problem can thus be solved in principle. Shanon concluded that the question should be *what is the computational effort of the cryptanalyst versus that of the legitimate user.*

Public-key cryptography differs from conventional cryptography in the way the key is used. While the same key is used for both encryption and decryption in conventional cryptography, this is not the case in public-key cryptography. There are two keys: The encryption key, and the decryption key. The decryption key is kept secret, while the encryption key is made public. Thus each user can encrypt messages. Without knowing the decryption key, however, messages sent by other users cannot be efficiently decrypted.

Public-key cryptography was proposed in 1976 by Diffie and Hellman in the seminal paper "New Directions in Cryptography" [20]. A few months later, the first two implementations of public-key cryptosystems were found: The Merkle–Hellman scheme [35] and the Rivest–Shamir–Adelman scheme [42]. These works related well-known complexity-theoretic questions, whose solution is believed to be intractable (like solving a 0-1 knapsack or factoring large numbers), to the difficulty of cryptanalysis. The relation between public-key cryptography and complexity theory is more obvious than the relation for conventional cryptography. Even without inspecting any ciphertext, the public encryption key determines at least one secret decryption key. This secret key enables everyone (in principle) to decrypt all messages efficiently. However, while this means that public-key cryptosystems are useless from the information theoretic point of view, things look brighter if one considers the amount of resources needed to carry out such an attack. It might well be infeasible to determine the decryption key within any reasonable computational effort.

Attacks other than finding the secret decryption key should also be considered. For example, it might be possible to decrypt certain ciphertexts without having the secret decryption key. Even the possibility of getting partial information about the contents of the plaintext without actually decrypting the ciphertext might be unacceptable in some circumstances. To overcome these potential difficulties, Goldwasser and Micali proposed a new type of randomized public-key cryptosystems in their "Probabilistic Encryption" paper [25]. They gave a concrete implementation for their scheme, based on the difficulty of deciding quadratic residuosity modulo composite numbers. The scheme randomly maps cleartext bits into a ciphertext block in a bit-by-bit fashion. An attractive property of this scheme is that an adversary with polynomially bounded resources cannot learn any partial information about the plaintext from the ciphertext. Thus a very strong measure of secrecy is achieved.

While such strong result cannot hold for *deterministic* encryption schemes, it is not hard to see that some predicates must still remain somewhat secure. More precisely, some predicates $B(x)$ which are efficiently computable given the cleartext x, cannot be computed given the ciphertext $E(x)$ with no error. Otherwise, E could be inverted everywhere by computing the bits of x one by one. This observation, however, does not rule out the possibility that all such predicates B can be efficiently computed with only a small error.

In the first part of this thesis we explore questions related to the security of partial information in the RSA cryptosystem. It is quite easy to see that the RSA cryptosystem does leak certain partial information. For example, the Jacobi symbols of the plaintext and the ciphertext are always the same. Since Jacobi symbols are easy to compute, this partial information is not at all hidden under the RSA. So, assuming that RSA is indeed hard, the question of demonstrating predicates, which are kept secret under RSA encryption, naturally arises.

The bits in the binary expansion of the plaintext provide a very simple candidate for such secure predicates. For example, there seems to be no easy way to recover the least significant bit of the plaintext from the ciphertext. Of course, extracting this bit cannot be any harder than recovering the plaintext from the ciphertext. Thus the approach taken is to reduce the problem of inverting RSA to that of successfully guessing the least significant bit of the plaintext from the ciphertext.

We start by giving with the formal setting for investigating bit security. Following the approach of Blum and Micali [7], probabilistic Cook reductions are used. We assume that we are given an oracle for the least significant bit, and attempt to invert RSA using this oracle. It turns out that the quality of the oracle makes things different - better oracles are easier to use, while flaky ones are harder, or even impossible, to handle. The extreme case is that of an oracle which is correct exactly one half of the time. Since such oracle could in fact be implemented using an unbiased coin, any successful reduction using it would indicate that RSA is easy to invert.

We continue by describing three reductions. We start with the most reliable oracle for the least significant bit – one that never errs, and show how it can be used in a binary search procedure for inverting RSA. Next, oracles which are correct more than seventy five percent of the times are handled, using a combination of a new sampling method together with a binary gcd procedure.

Finally, we introduce the technique of two points based sampling. This technique allows efficient reduction even if the least significant bit oracle is only slightly better than a random coin toss. The reduction implies that the following two problems are equivalent (each is probabilistic polynomial-time reducible to the other):

1) Given the RSA encryption of a message, retrieve the message.

2) Given the RSA encryption of a message, guess the least-significant bit of the message with success probability $\frac{1}{2} + \frac{1}{poly(n)}$ (where n is the length of the RSA modulus).

This equivalence means that an adversary, given the ciphertext, cannot have a non-negligible advantage (over a random coin flip) in guessing the least-significant bit of the plaintext, unless he can break RSA.

We conclude the first part by extending these results to the simultaneous security of several least significant bits, and to the Rabin encryption function [39]. Applications to probabilistic encryption and to efficient generation of pseudo-random number generators [7] are also described.

A different line of research in public-key cryptography has dealt with the efficient cryptanalysis of the Merkle–Hellman cryptosystems. In 1982 Shamir [45] showed how to break the basic Merkle–Hellman cryptosystem. This work has led the way to attacks on more sophisticated versions of the Merkle–Hellman cryptosystem. In particular, Brickell [12] found a way to break the general Merkle–Hellman scheme, and Lagarias and Odlyzko [31] developed a technique which seems to threaten the security of any knapsack-type public-key cryptosystem having certain low density properties.

The second part of the thesis describes a new knapsack type public key cryptosystem which has a high density. The system is based on a construction of Bose and Chowla in finite fields arithmetic. This construction yields dense sequences of integers, with the property that all subset sums are distinct. (More precisely, all subset sums for subsets not exceeding a certain size.) This is an appropriate starting point for building a knapsack type public-key cryptosystem, since the property of unique decryption is guaranteed.

Certain difficulties have to be overcome to make this idea work. First, the decryption must be made efficient given all the information at the disposal of the system constructor. Once this is done, we have to make a public-key cryptosystem out of the construction. Some information must be kept secret to prevent decryption by users other than the legitimate receiver. Finally, an efficient way of generating the keys should be given. In our case, in order to compute the keys, one has to take discrete logarithms in the finite field $GF(p^h)$. While no efficient algorithms for this problem are known in general, some particular cases can be handled in practice. These cases provide the practical basis for the new cryptosystem. We give detailed description of implementing the scheme and propose concrete parameters.

Finally, we examine some possible cryptanalytic attacks against the new cryptosystem. We argue that the new cryptosystem resists these specific attacks (i.e. these attacks are infeasible for the proposed parameters). However, we are not able to prove that this cryptosystem is unbreakable, and leave its security as an open problem. We conclude by presenting a specific instance of the cryptosystem, whose cryptanalysis is proposed as a challenge to the would-be cryptanalyst.

Part I

RSA Bit Security

Chapter 2

Background

This chapter serves to provide technical background for the first part of the thesis. The RSA function and its properties are examined. Next, the formal framework for studying bit security is given. Throughout the thesis, when we say that something is easy to compute, we mean that it can be computed in (deterministic or probabilistic) polynomial time as a function of its arguments.

2.1 The RSA Cryptosystem

In this section we introduce some notation which will be used throughout the first part. We proceed by reviewing the definition of the RSA encryption and some of its properties.

Definition 2.1.1: *Let N be a natural number. Z_N will denote the ring of integers modulo N, where addition and multiplication are done modulo N.*

It would be convenient to view the elements of Z_N as points on a circle (see figure 2.1). Throughout the thesis, $n = \log_2 N$ will denote the length of the modulus N. All algorithms we'll discuss have inputs of length $O(n)$.

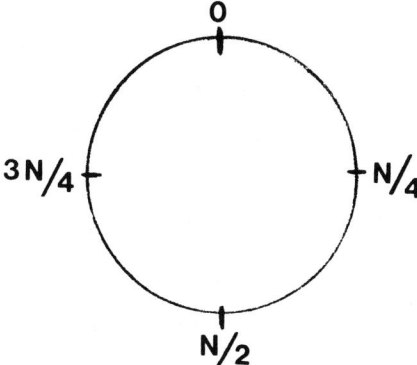

Fig. 2.1 – Cyclic representation of Z_N

Definition 2.1.2: Let N be a natural number, and x an integer. $[x]_N$ will denote the remainder of x modulo N (notice that for all x, $0 \leq [x]_N < N$).

Let p, q be two large primes, and $N = pq$ be their product. The *RSA encryption function* is operating in the message space Z_N, where N is of the above form. The encryption of x is $E_N(x) \stackrel{\text{def}}{=} [x^e]_N$, where e is relatively prime to $\varphi(N) = (p-1)(q-1)$. The numbers N and e are put in a public file and thus any user can encrypt messages with them. Exponentiation is efficiently computed by, for example, the successive squaring method [29, p. 441]. Below, we explain how the RSA decryption works. This is not necessary for the rest of this thesis and is given here only for the sake of completeness.

The integers in the range $[0, N-1]$ which are relatively prime to N constitute a group under multiplication modulo N. This group is denoted by Z_N^*. The number of elements in this group is $\varphi(N) = (p-1)(q-1)$. By Lagrange theorem, for every $x \in Z_N^*$, if $a \equiv 0 \pmod{\varphi(N)}$, then $x^a \equiv 1 \pmod{N}$ (since the group contains $\varphi(N)$ elements). Let e be relatively prime to $\varphi(N)$. Then there is another integer d which satisfies $ed \equiv 1 \pmod{\varphi(N)}$. Every $x \in Z_N^*$ satisfies $(x^e)^d = x^{ed} = x \bmod N$. Given e and $\varphi(N)$, d can easily be found, using the extended Euclidean algorithm [29]. However, knowing N and e but not $\varphi(N)$, finding d is equivalent to factoring N. In the RSA cryptosystem, the public encryption key consists of N and e, while d is the secret decryption key. To encrypt a message $x \in Z_N^*$, the user computes $E_N(x) = [x^e]_N$. To decrypt $y = E_N(x)$, the legitimate receiver computes $[y^d]_N = E_N(x)^d \bmod N$. By the identity above, this gives the original message x. Messages in $Z_N - Z_N^*$ are not of special concern since any of them (except 0) enables the factorization of N and hence are not likely to be found (unless factoring N is easy). For this reason, we will not be particularly careful to distinguish between Z_N and Z_N^*.

2.2 Multiplicative and Additive Properties of the RSA

Viewed as a function from Z_N into itself, the RSA is a multiplicative function, namely $E_N(xy) = E_N(x)E_N(y)$. Thus if we have an encryption $E_N(x)$ together with an element $r \in Z_N$, it is easy to compute $E_N(rx)$, even without knowing x: First compute $E_N(r)$, and then multiply $E_N(x)$ by $E_N(r)$ modulo N. For every

x, multiplication by x is a one-to-one operation in Z_N^*. Given $E_N(x)$, if r is chosen with uniform probability distribution from Z_N^* then rx is uniformly distributed in Z_N^*. Thus it is easy to compute $E_N(rx)$ with r known and uniformly distributed. A useful observation on the difficulty of inverting RSA follows: A $T(n)$-time algorithm for inverting RSA on a subset $S \subset Z_N$ of density $\gamma = |S|/N$ implies a $T(n)\gamma^{-1}$ expected time algorithm for inverting RSA on the whole range Z_N. Given $E_N(x)$, map it at random into Z_N by computing $E_N(rx)$. With probability γ^{-1}, $rx \in S$ will hold. But in such case $E_N(rx)$ can be inverted. To recover x from rx, multiply rx by r^{-1} modulo N.

The situation with respect to addition is quite different. Given $E_N(x)$ and r, it is not at all clear that $E_N(r+x)$ can be found. In fact, for small exponents e, the problem of computing $E_N(x+r)$ is equivalent to the problem of inverting $E_N(x)$. As an example, consider the case with $e = 3$. Suppose we have an oracle which, given $E_N(x)$ and r, returns

$$E_N(r+x) = [(r+x)^3]_N = [r^3 + 3r^2x + 3rx^2 + x^3]_N \ .$$

Feeding the same oracle with $E_N(x)$ and $2r$, we'll get

$$[(2r+x)^3]_N = [8r^3 + 12r^2x + 6rx^2 + x^3]_N \ .$$

Subtracting multiples of $[r^3]_N$ and $[x^3]_N$ (which we have) from both equations, and dividing by 3, we are left with two equations over Z_N

$$r^2x + rx^2 = a,$$
$$4r^2x + 2rx^2 = b,$$

where a, b, r are known. The quadratic term in x can be eliminated, and we are left with a linear equation in x which is easily solved over Z_N. In general, this procedure will be polynomial in e (and not in its length) and so is efficient only for small exponents e.

While the last paragraph indicates that, given $E_N(x)$, we cannot hope to come up with pairs $E_N(s)$, $E_N(s+x)$ with s known and uniformly distributed, we can get such pairs if we omit the requirement that s be known. To achieve this, recall that if r is uniformly distributed, so is $[rx]_N$. Since $(r+1)x = rx+x$, we can compute both $E_N(rx)$ and $E_N(rx+x)$. Substituting $s = rx$, we get a pair with the desired properties. (Notice that for a single element it would not mean much to ask for $E_N(sx)$ with s uniformly distributed but unknown.)

2.3 Predicate Security

In this section we give definitions for the notion that a bit (or, more generally, a Boolean predicate) is well hidden under an encryption function. The formal framework is that of polynomial-time probabilistic Cook reductions. This approach follows the work of Blum and Micali [7].

Definition 2.3.1: *Let $B(x)$ be a Boolean predicate, defined on the elements of Z_N. Let $\mathcal{O}_N$ be a probabilistic oracle which, given $E_N(x)$, outputs a guess, $\mathcal{O}_N(E_N(x))$, for $B(x)$ (this guess might depend on the internal coin tosses of $\mathcal{O}_N$). Let $\varepsilon(\cdot)$ be a function from integers into the interval $[0, \frac{1}{2}]$. Recall that n denotes the length of N. We say that $\mathcal{O}_N$ is a $\varepsilon(n)$-oracle for B if the probability that the oracle is correct, given $E_N(x)$ as its input, is at least $\frac{1}{2} + \varepsilon(n)$. The probability space is that of all $x \in Z_N$ and all $0-1$ sequences of internal coin tosses, with uniform distribution.*

To clarify the definition, notice that very different oracles can be $\varepsilon(n)$-oracles for some predicate B. Two extreme examples are an oracle which is deterministic (i.e. always outputs the same answer when given $E_N(x)$ as input) and is correct on $\frac{1}{2} + \varepsilon(n)$ of the x's, versus an oracle which is "totally probabilistic" – gives the correct answer with probability $\frac{1}{2} + \varepsilon(n)$ for every x. It turns out that the second type of oracle is relatively well behaved, while the first type can be quite obnoxious. Nevertheless, the theorems we'll prove will only be sensitive to $\varepsilon(n)$ and not to the inner structure of the oracle (which is hard to analyze). A second comment on the definition is the reason for restricting it to oracles which succeed with probability at least $\frac{1}{2}$. Oracles with success probability less than $\frac{1}{2}$ can be transformed to oracles of the above type by reversing their answers.

Definition 2.3.2: *We say that the Boolean predicate B is $\varepsilon(n)$-secure if there is a probabilistic polynomial time algorithm which inverts E_N, using an arbitrary $\varepsilon(n)$-oracle $\mathcal{O}_N$ for B.*

A Boolean predicate is $\frac{1}{2}$ secure if a totally reliable oracle for B can be used to invert RSA in probabilistic polynomial time. It is $\frac{1}{4}$ secure if any oracle which is correct in seventy five percent of its answers can be used to invert RSA in probabilistic polynomial time. Since we only required probabilistic polynomial time reductions, it is conceivable that a reduction for $\frac{1}{4}$ oracles is slower than a reduction for totally reliable oracle. Notice, however, that such reduction should run for *any* $\frac{1}{4}$ oracle in expected time n^c for some $c > 0$, and c cannot depend on the oracle (a reduction might run for less than n^c for certain $\frac{1}{4}$ oracles, but n^c should be an absolute upper bound).

Definition 2.3.3: Let $B_1(\cdot), B_2(\cdot)$ be two Boolean predicates, defined on the elements of Z_N. We say that B_1 is RSA reducible to B_2 if there is a probabilistic polynomial time oracle procedure P^O which satisfies: For every $0 \leq \varepsilon(n) \leq \frac{1}{2}$ and every $\varepsilon(n)$-oracle O for B_2, P^O is an $\varepsilon(n)$-oracle for B_1.

This definition is similar to the standard definition of probabilistic polynomial time Cook reductions. The difference is that instead of being fed with the argument x, the procedure is given the encryption $E_N(x)$. Thus it should perform the reduction "blindfolded". Of course, if RSA is easy to invert than the last definition becomes identical to the standard one.

Definition 2.3.4: Let $B_1(\cdot), B_2(\cdot)$ be two Boolean predicate, defined on the elements of Z_N. We say that B_1 and B_2 are RSA equivalent if each is RSA reducible to the other.

It is possible to give more restrictive definitions (e.g. insist on deterministic reductions) or more general ones (e.g. allowing some degradation in output quality due to the reduction), but we will not do it here. The main reason for introducing the notion of RSA reducibility is that it allows to derive predicate security for one predicate by using results for another predicate. This is stated formally in the following lemma.

Lemma 2.3.5: Let $B_1(\cdot), B_2(\cdot)$ be two Boolean predicate, defined on the elements of Z_N. If B_2 is RSA reducible to B_1, and B_2 is $\varepsilon(n)$-secure, then B_1 is also $\varepsilon(n)$-secure.

2.4 Some Predicates and Reductions Among Them

In this section we introduce some notation and define the parity predicate, $par_N(\cdot)$, and the $half_N(\cdot)$ predicate. We then show that $half_N$ is RSA equivalent to the least significant bit.

Definition 2.4.1: For $0 \leq x < N$, $L_N(x)$ denotes the least-significant bit in the binary representation of x.

Definition 2.4.2: Let x be an integer. We define

$$abs_N(x) = \begin{cases} [x]_N & \text{if } [x]_N < \frac{N}{2}; \\ N - [x]_N & \text{otherwise.} \end{cases}$$

Pictorially, $abs(x)$ can be viewed as the distance from $[x]_N$ to 0 on the Z_N circle (see figure 2.). Notice that $abs_N(x) = abs_N(-x)$.

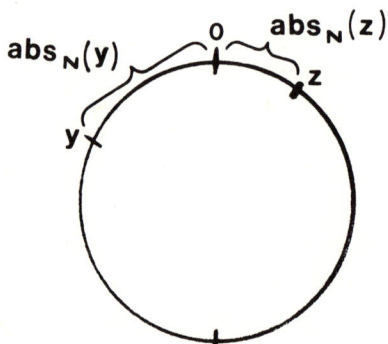

Fig. 2.2 – The abs_N function.

Definition 2.4.3: The parity of x, $par_N(x)$, is defined as the least-significant bit of $abs_N(x)$.

Since abs_N is symmetric with respect to 0, so is par_N. For example, $par_N(N-3) = par_N(3) = 1$. The parity predicate and its relation to the least significant bit will play a crucial role in the next chapters.

Definition 2.4.4: *The predicate $half_N(\cdot)$ is defined by*

$$half_N(x) = \begin{cases} top, & \text{if } \frac{N}{2} < x < N; \\ bottom, & \text{otherwise.} \end{cases}$$

Lemma 2.4.5: *L_N and $half_N$ are RSA equivalent.*

Proof. We use the fact that N is odd, which implies that division by 2 is well defined and a one-to-one operation in Z_N^*. If $L_N(x) = 0$ then x is even and therefore dividing it by 2 over Z_N^* coincides with division by 2 over the integers. But in such a case, $0 \leq x < N$ implies $0 \leq \frac{x}{2} < \frac{N}{2}$. Hence $L_N(x) = 0$ implies $half_N(x/2) =$ bottom. Since exactly half the elements are mapped to *bottom* elements, the rest must be mapped to *top* elements. We thus get $L_N(x) = 0$ iff $half_N(x/2) =$ bottom.

Thus, given a $\varepsilon(n)$-oracle $\mathcal{O}_\mathcal{L}$ for the least significant bit, we construct a $\varepsilon(n)$-oracle $\mathcal{O}_\mathcal{H}$ for the $half_N$ predicate by taking the input $E_N(x)$, computing $E_N(2x) = E_N(2)E_N(x)$, and feeding $E_N(2x)$ to $\mathcal{O}_\mathcal{L}$. If $\mathcal{O}_\mathcal{L}$ replies $L_N(2x) = 0$ then we output $half_N(x) =$ bottom, otherwise we output $half_N(x) =$ top.

Conversely, given a $\varepsilon(n)$-oracle $\mathcal{O}_\mathcal{H}$ for the $half_N$ predicate, we construct a $\varepsilon(n)$-oracle $\mathcal{O}_\mathcal{L}$ for the least significant bit, by taking the input $E_N(x)$, computing $E_N(x/2) = E_N(2^{-1})E_N(x) = E(\frac{N+1}{2})E(x)$, and feeding $E_N(x/2)$ to $\mathcal{O}_\mathcal{H}$. If the reply is $half_N(x/2) =$ bottom then we output $L_N(x) = 0$, otherwise we output $L_N(x) = 1$.

Clearly both reductions are in polynomial time, and the reliability of the resulting oracle is equal to the reliability of the original oracle. □

CHAPTER 3

VERY RELIABLE ORACLES

In this chapter we investigate the use of very reliable oracles for the $half_N$ predicate. Using deterministic reductions, we demonstrate $\frac{1}{2}$-security for this predicate. We then switch our attention to reliable oracles for the least significant bit, and investigate the *statistical* information which can be derived from them.

3.1 Binary Search Inversion

In this section we investigate reliable oracles for the $half_N$ predicate. We show how to use them in a binary search procedure for inverting RSA. The results in this section were obtained independently by Goldwasser, Micali and Tong [26].

Theorem 3.1.1: $half_N$ is $\frac{1}{2}$-secure.

Proof. Let $\mathcal{O}_\mathcal{H}$ be a $\frac{1}{2}$ oracle for the $half_N$ predicate. By the definition, this means that given as input $E_N(x)$, $\mathcal{O}_\mathcal{H}$ outputs the correct answer for $half_N(x)$. The answer of $\mathcal{O}_\mathcal{H}$ restricts the possible interval in which x might fall to half the original space. Suppose, for example, that $half_N(x) = top$. Thus $\frac{N}{2} \leq x \leq N$. As an integer, $2x$ must therefore be in the interval $[N, 2N]$. Reduction modulo N shifts this interval back to $[0, N]$. Thus if $half_N(2x) = bottom$, we can infer that over the integers, $N \leq 2x \leq \frac{3N}{2}$. This, in turn, restricts the possible interval for x to $\frac{N}{2} \leq x \leq \frac{3N}{4}$, an interval of length $\frac{N}{4}$ (see figure 3.1).

By querying $\mathcal{O}_\mathcal{H}$ with $E_N(x), E_N(2x) \ldots, E_N(2^i x), \ldots$ (for $i = 0, 1, \ldots, \log_2 N$) we get the (correct) answers for $half_N(x), half_N(2x), \ldots, half_N(2^i x), \ldots$. We can thus perform a binary search for x: Start with a "possible interval" $P_0 = [0, N]$, and narrow it by a factor of 2 after every query. If the remaining interval before the i-th query was $P_i = [\frac{l}{2^i} N, \frac{l+1}{2^i} N]$, then after the i-th query we are left with

$$P_{i+1} = \begin{cases} [\frac{2l}{2^{i+1}} N, \frac{2l+1}{2^{i+1}} N], & \text{if } half_N(2^i x) = bottom; \\ [\frac{2l}{2^{i+1}} N, \frac{2l+2}{2^{i+1}} N], & \text{otherwise.} \end{cases}$$

After $n = \lceil \log_2 N \rceil$ queries, P_n is narrowed down to a length 1 interval, which must contain x. □

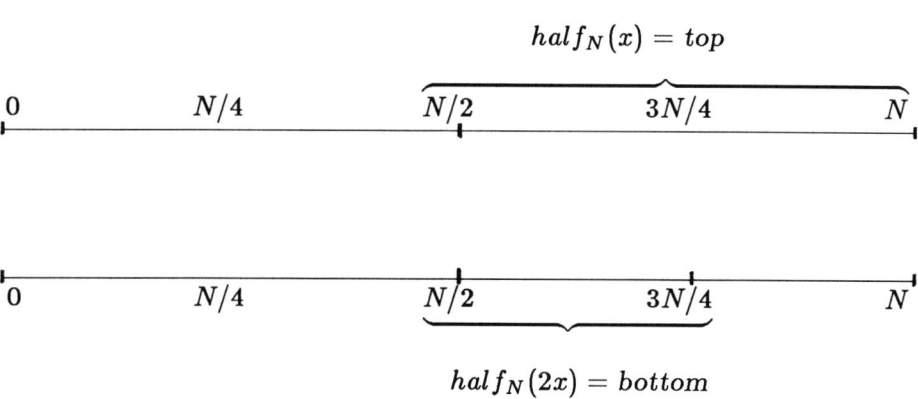

Fig. 3.1 – Possible position after two queries.

The reliability of $\mathcal{O}_{\mathcal{H}}$ was crucial for this proof. A single incorrect answer throws us to the wrong interval. However, the proof can be modified to tolerate any $\frac{1}{2} - \frac{\alpha}{n}$ oracle ($\alpha < 1$ a constant). To demonstrate the basic idea of the modification, assume that the oracle is deterministic. In that case, being a $\frac{1}{2} - \frac{\alpha}{n}$ oracle means that $\mathcal{O}_{\mathcal{H}}$ gives the correct answer for at least $1 - \frac{\alpha}{n}$ of all Z_N elements. Since for every input $E_N(x)$, $\mathcal{O}_{\mathcal{H}}$ is queried exactly n times, the density of elements for which *some* error occurs is no greater than α. Thus the above procedure will be successful in inverting E_N on at least a $1 - \alpha$ fraction of all inputs. By the observation in section 2.2, this implies a probabilistic polynomial-time algorithm for inverting RSA (given access to such oracle). However, this technique works only for $\frac{1}{2} - O\left(\frac{1}{n}\right)$ oracles.

Using the equivalence between the least significant bit and $half_N$, theorem 1 implies the following:

Corollary 3.1.2: *The least significant bit is $\frac{1}{2}$-secure.*

This corollary means that RSA can be inverted in polynomial time, given an error-free oracle for the least significant bit.

3.2 Parity Information From Reliable Least Significant Bit Oracle.

In view of the limitations in the inverting method of the previous section, we develop here a different one. This method will enable us to determine the parity of x, $par_N(x)$, for arguments x which are close to 0 mod N. In the following chapter we will explain how to invert RSA, given access to such parity subroutine. The intuitive idea is to infer $par_N(x)$ for any "small" x by comparing the least significant bit of s with that of $s + x$, where s is chosen at random in Z_N. If both bits are the same, the hypothesis $par_N(x) = 0$ is supported, while if they are different then $par_N(x) = 1$ is supported.

We would find it convenient to switch the emphasis to oracles for the least significant bit, $\mathcal{O}_\mathcal{L}$. The way these oracles will be used here is different than that of the previous section – instead of gaining deterministic information (which interval x belongs to), we are now going to gain statistical information. This information will depend on our good luck, or rather on the lack of bad luck. However, using the laws of large numbers, this statistical information is as useful as deterministic one.

For the rest of this section, we assume that the (unknown) x is "not too large", namely $abs_N(x) < \delta N$ for some constant $\delta \leq \frac{1}{4}$. Using the cyclic representation of Z_N, we say that a wraparound 0 occurs when x is added to s if s and $s + x$ are on opposite sides of 0.

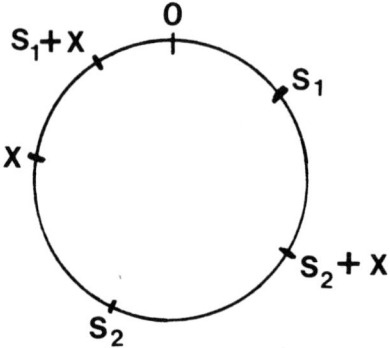

Fig. 3.2 – Wraparound $(s_1, s_1 + x)$, and no wraparound $(s_2, s_2 + x)$.

More precisely, wraparound occurs for a "positive" x ($abs_N(x) = x$) iff $N - abs_N(x) < s < N$, and for a "negative" x iff $0 < s < abs_N(x)$. In either case, if s is chosen at random in Z_N, then the probability of a wraparound 0 when x is added to s is exactly $abs_N(x)/N$. Since $abs_N(x) < \delta N$, this probability is bounded above by $\delta \leq \frac{1}{4}$. If no wrap-around occurs, the parity of x is equal to 0 if the least-significant bits of s and $s + x$ are identical, and equal to 1 otherwise. Thus if s is chosen in Z_N with uniform probability distribution, then the conditional probability that $par_N(x) = 0$, given that $\mathcal{O}_\mathcal{L}$ answers the same on $E_N(s), E_N(s+x)$, is at least $1 - \delta \geq 3/4$ (and similarly for $par_N(x) = 1$ given different answers). To generate pairs $E_N(s), E_N(s+x)$ with s uniformly distributed, the trick of section 2.2 is used. We call a single pair query of $\mathcal{O}_\mathcal{L}$ a x *measurment*. From the discussion above, a single x measurment indicates the parity of x correctly with probability $\geq 3/4$. To improve the reliability of the result, several independent x measurments are performed, and the indication given by their majority is taken.

Code for parity subroutine with parameter m.

```
1.    procedure PARITY(x):
2.    INPUT ← E_N(x)
3.        count_0 ← 0
4.        count_1 ← 0
5.        for i ← 1 to m do
6.            pick r_i ∈ Z_N at random
7.            if O_L (E_N(r_i x)) = O_L (E_N(r_i x + x))
8.            then count_0 ← count_0 + 1
9.            else count_1 ← count_1 + 1
10.       od
11.       if count_0 > count_1
12.       then return par_N(x) = 0
13.       else return par_N(x) = 1
```

If the m random points r_i are chosen independently, then with probability $1 - 2^{-\theta(m)}$, the majority of the measurements will give the correct answer. This can be easily proved using the Chernoff bound [41, p. 387]). A detailed proof (using even less reliable oracles) can be found in chapter 4. If the r_i's are not mutually independent, but just pairwise independent, then the answer is correct with probability at least $1 - O\left(\frac{1}{m}\right)$. A proof of this statement, based on Chebyshev's inequality, can be found in chapter 5. This weaker version will be crucial in proving the strong security result.

Chapter 4

Inverting with a Reliable Parity Subroutine

In the first section we give a high level description of our future plan. This is followed by what might otherwise seem to be unrelated – an examination of the Brent–Kung gcd procedure, its properties, and running time. In the third section we show how to implement the Brent–Kung gcd procedure on messages, using as data only encrypted messages, provided that a reliable parity subroutine is available. We continue by demonstrating that the parity subroutine of chapter 3 can be reliably implemented even if the least significant bit oracle $\mathcal{O}_\mathcal{L}$ can err. Finally, a quantitative analysis of the error gives a $\frac{1}{4} + \frac{1}{poly(n)}$ security result for the least significant bit.

4.1 General Plan

Given $E_N(x)$, we would like to find x. The parity subroutine of the last chapter supplies $par_N(x)$ when x is not too big and $\mathcal{O}_\mathcal{L}$ is very reliable. As we'll see later, it is possible to implement exactly the same subroutine even if $\mathcal{O}_\mathcal{L}$ is not that reliable, provided that x is restricted to be of smaller absolute value. So far, this is not a severe restriction, because even if the original x did not have this property, we can get a known multiple of it, ax, which is small (this will happen with reasonable probability, but at this point there is no way to verify that it indeed happened). The question is what do we do with this bit of information?

If $par_N(x) = 0$, we can divide x by 2. If x is small, so is $x/2$. Therefore the parity subroutine will give the correct answer about $par_N(x/2)$ as well. But unless x is a power of 2 (or 'almost' one), this process will be stopped the first time the parity returns 1 as its answer. If we go on dividing by 2, the result will not be small, and thus the parity subroutine will give the wrong answer if asked again. To make progress, we *must* keep the arguments small.

Suppose we start with two random multiples of x, $[ax]_N$ and $[bx]_N$, both small. When computing gcd, the intermediate numbers involved only become smaller. If the gcd makes only parity tests, and could be implemented even when the arguments are encrypted, then we have a chance to invert.

4.2 Brent–Kung GCD

Both classical and binary [29, p. 321] gcd algorithms find the gcd of two n-bit integers in $O(n)$ iterations. To find the gcd both require tests of the form 'is $b < c$?', which we do not know how to do if b and c are encrypted. For this reason we need a modified version of the binary gcd algorithm, one which makes no such tests. The specific version given here is from Brent and Kung [9], and was used to efficiently implement gcd in a systolic array. (The main advantage of this version is that only the least significant bits should be looked at in order to perform the parity checks. This is a desired feature when the bits are spread across the systolic array.) The Brent–Kung method is faster than the one which was used originally in [3].

1. **procedure** PLUS MINUS gcd:
    $\{\, a \text{ odd},\, b \neq 0,\, |a|, |b| \leq 2^n \,\}$
2.   INPUT $\leftarrow a, b$
3. $\alpha \leftarrow n$
4. $\beta \leftarrow n$
5.   **repeat**
6.   **while** parity$(b) = 0$ **do**
7. $b \leftarrow b/2$
8. $\beta \leftarrow \beta - 1$
9.   **od**
    $\{b \text{ odd}, |b| \leq 2^\beta\}$
10.   **if** $\beta \leq \alpha$ **then** swap (a,b), swap (α, β)
    $\{\alpha \leq \beta, |a| \leq 2^\alpha, |b| \leq 2^\beta;\ a \text{ and } b \text{ odd}\}$
11.   **if** parity$\left(\frac{a+b}{2}\right) = 0$ **then** $b \leftarrow \frac{a+b}{2}$ **else** $b \leftarrow \frac{a-b}{2}$
    $\{b \text{ even}, |b| \leq 2^\beta\}$
12.   **until** $b = 0$
13.   **return** gcd $= a$

This algorithm returns the gcd of its input provided that a is odd and $b \neq 0$. Its correctness under this condition follows from the fact that if b is even and a is odd, then $\gcd(a,b) = \gcd(a, \frac{b}{2})$, while if both b and a are odd then

$\gcd(a,b) = \gcd(a, \frac{a+b}{2}) = \gcd(a, \frac{a-b}{2})$. The assertions in braces simplify the run time analysis: In every repeat loop (except the first one if b was odd to begin with) the sum $\alpha + \beta$ decreases by at least 1. Therefore the number of loops is at most $2n + 1$. Each time a parity is checked in line 6 of the code and is found to be 0, $\alpha + \beta$ decrease by 1. The only other place where parity is checked is in line 11 of the code, and this happens once per repeat loop. Thus there are no more than 2 parity checks per loop where the sum $\alpha + \beta$ remains unchanged. Therefore the total number of parity checks per gcd invocation is at most $3(2n + 1) = 6n + 3 = O(n)$.

4.3 GCD Inversion Using a Parity Subroutine

Given an encrypted message, $E_N(x)$, the plaintext x is reconstructed as follows. First, two random multiples of $E_N(x)$, $E_N(ax)$ and $E_N(bx)$, are computed. A Brent–Kung gcd procedure is applied to $[ax]_N$ and $[bx]_N$. This gcd procedure uses a parity subroutine which we assume to give correct answers. Even though neither $[ax]_N$ nor $[bx]_N$ are explicitly known, we can manipulate them via their encryption. In particular, we can compute the encryption of any linear combination $A[ax]_N + B[bx]_N$ when both A, B are known. When the gcd procedure terminates, we get a representation of $\gcd([ax]_N, [bx]_N)$ in the form $[lx]_N$, where l and $E_N(lx)$ are known. If $[ax]_N$ and $[bx]_N$ are relatively prime, then $[lx]_N = 1$. This fact can be detected since $E_N(1) = 1$. Therefore, $x \equiv l^{-1} \pmod{N}$ can be easily computed and verified (by comparing $E_N(l^{-1})$ to $E_N(x)$).

```
1.     procedure gcd INVERSION :
2.     INPUT ← E_N(x)
;      Randomization
3.     Pick a,b ∈ Z_N at random. Compute E_N(ax), E_N(bx)
;      Brent-Kung gcd of [ax]_N, [bx]_N
       {z_1 = [ax]_N, z_2 = [bx]_N}
4.     α ← n,
5.     β ← n
6.     count ← 0
8.         repeat
9.             while par_N(bx) = 0 do
10.                b ← [b/2]_N
                  {gcd([ax]_N, [bx]_N) = gcd(z_1, z_2)}
11.                β ← β − 1
```

```
12.                    count ← count+1
13.                    if count> 6n + 3 then go to 3
14.               od
15.               if β ≤ α then swap (a, b), swap(α, β)
16.               if par_N(ax+bx/2) = 0
17.                    then  b ← [a+b/2]_N
18.                    else  b ← [a-b/2]_N
                       {gcd([ax]_N, [bx]_N) = gcd(z_1, z_2)}
19.               count ← count+1
20.               if count> 6n + 3 then go to 3
21.       until b = 0
;    Inverting
22.  if E_N(ax) ≠ (−1)^σ then go to 3
23.  x ← [(−1)^σ a^{−1}]_N
24.  return x.
```

The test in line 22 of the code makes sure that the algorithm never errs. The assertions in the braces guarantee that if the parity subroutine does not err, then the gcd of the current $[ax]_N, [bx]_N$ is invariant. Combining this with the claims in the previous section, we can conclude that if the original pair $[ax]_N, [bx]_N$ is relatively prime and the parity subroutine answered correctly on all queries, the algorithm will retrieve x. To analyze the expected run time we need to know the probability that two randomly chosen integers with absolute value not exceeding N are relatively prime. A famous theorem of Dirichlet [29, p. 324] states that this probability converges to $\frac{6}{\pi^2}$ as N tends to ∞. This can be intuitively (but not rigorously) seen if we notice that for two numbers to be relatively prime, they should not be divisible by the same prime. For any prime p, the probability that p divides both numbers is $\frac{1}{p^2}$. If these probabilities are independent for different primes, then the probability that no prime divides both numbers is $\prod\left(1 - \frac{1}{p^2}\right)$. The inverse of this infinite product is

$$\prod_p \frac{1}{1 - 1/p^2} = \prod_p \left(1 + \frac{1}{p^2} + \frac{1}{p^4} + \ldots\right) = \sum_{n=1}^{\infty} \frac{1}{n^2} = \frac{\pi^2}{6}.$$

Returning to the gcd inversion, the variable *count* guarantees that even if the parity subroutine occasionally errs, we will not run into an infinite loop in a single gcd iteration. We saw that if the parity subroutine gives correct answers, then $6n + 3$ is an absolute upper bound on the number of parity checks. Thus if this bound is exceeded, something must have gone wrong and we better start again.

The probability that x will be retrieved in any single gcd attempt is thus

$$\frac{6}{\pi^2} \cdot \Pr(ax \text{ and } bx \text{ are small})$$

$$\cdot \Pr(\text{all answers of the parity subroutine were correct}) \;.$$

In the next section we'll show that if the least significant bit oracle $\mathcal{O}_\mathcal{L}$ queried by the parity subroutine is a $\frac{1}{4} + \frac{1}{poly(n)}$ oracle, the later probability can be made to be greater than $\frac{1}{2}$, with only polynomially many oracle queries.

4.4 Reliable Parity Subroutine with $\frac{1}{4} + \frac{1}{poly(n)}$ Oracle

The parity subroutine of section 3.2 was analyzed under the assumption that $\mathcal{O}_\mathcal{L}$ is a $\frac{1}{2}$ oracle. If, instead, it is just a $\frac{1}{4} + \varepsilon(n)$ oracle, the analysis becomes somewhat different (but the code is not changed).

The parity subroutine is called with $E_N(dx)$, where d is given. Let us redefine "small" and say that dx is small if $abs_N(dx) < N \cdot \varepsilon(n)$. We will show that the parity subroutine determines $par_N(dx)$ correctly (with overwhelming probability), provided dx is small. Recall that $\mathcal{O}_\mathcal{L}(E_N(y))$ is the oracle's guess for $L_N(y)$, the least significant bit of $[y]_N$. If no wraparound occurs, and the oracle is correct on both $[rx]_N$ and $[rx + dx]_N$ (i.e. $\mathcal{O}_\mathcal{L}(E_N(rx)) = L_N(rx)$ and $\mathcal{O}_\mathcal{L}(E_N(rx + dx)) = L_N(rx + dx)$), then the outcome of this dx-measurement is correct. Since dx is small, the probability of wraparound is at most $\varepsilon(n)$. Wraparounds are not likely for small dx and so the main source of errors in the parity subroutine is the errors of the oracle. A dx-measurement may be wrong if the oracle errs on either end points ($[rx]_N$, $[rx+dx]_N$). As both $[rx]_N$, $[rx+dx]_N$ are uniformly distributed in Z_N, the error probability of a dx-measurement is at most twice the error probability of the oracle. The error probability of the oracle is $\frac{1}{4} - \varepsilon(n)$, so the probability that the oracle's answer on one or both points is *wrong* is at most $\frac{1}{2} - 2\varepsilon(n)$. (It is not true that the correctness of the oracle answers on $[rx]_N$ and $[rx+dx]_N$ are independent. Thus we only bound the error in any of these two events by the sum of the two error probabilities.) Accounting for both sources of possible errors, this implies that, for small dx, the error probability in a single dx-measurement is at most $\frac{1}{2} - 2\varepsilon(n) + \varepsilon(n) = \frac{1}{2} - \varepsilon(n)$.

The above estimate holds for any single dx measurment. Picking mutually independent r_i ($i = 1, 2, \ldots m$), the m dx measurments are independent events. The *majority* of all measurments will indicate the correct parity of dx with better probability than the individual experiments. In order to estimate the probability that the majority of these k measurments will give the wrong answer, we use the Chernoff Bound [41, ch. VII, sec. 4, Th. 2]: Let $\varsigma_1, \varsigma_2, \ldots, \varsigma_m$ be independent zero-one random variables with $Pr(\varsigma_i = 1) = p$, where $p \leq 1/2$. Then for all $0 < \delta \leq p(1-p)$ we have

$$Pr\left(\frac{1}{m} \cdot \left|\sum_{i=1}^{m}(\varsigma_i - p)\right| \geq \delta\right) \leq 2 \cdot \exp\left[-\frac{m\delta^2}{2p(1-p)\left(1 + \frac{\delta}{2p(1-p)}\right)^2}\right] \quad (*)$$

In our case, we define $\varsigma_i = 1$ if the i-th measurement gives a wrong answer, so $p \leq \frac{1}{2} - \varepsilon(n)$. The majority points to the wrong direction iff $\left(\frac{1}{m}\sum_{i=1}^{m}\varsigma_i \geq \frac{1}{2}\right)$. Since $Pr\left(\frac{1}{m}\sum_{i=1}^{m}\varsigma_i \geq \frac{1}{2}\right) \leq \frac{1}{m} \cdot \sum_{i=1}^{m}(\varsigma_i - p) \geq \varepsilon(n)$, it suffices to bound this last expression. In our case, the right-hand side of the inequality (*) is $\leq 2 \cdot e^{-m\delta^2/2}$. Substituting $m = 2\varepsilon^{-2}(n) \cdot \log_e 26n$, the error probability is no more than $2 \cdot e^{-m\delta^2/2} < 1/13n$.

If dx is small and the parity subroutine returns the correct $par_N(dx)$, then the next $d'x$ will also be small. Thus if the original $[ax]_N$ and $[bx]_N$ were small to begin with, and the parity subroutine does not err, then it is only called with small arguments during the the gcd computation. The probability that $[ax]_N, [bx]_N$ are both small and relatively prime is at least $\varepsilon^2(n)/2$. Under these conditions, the probability of no error in all $6n + 3$ calls of the parity subroutine is at least $1 - \frac{6n+3}{13n} > \frac{1}{2}$. Thus the overall probability that x is recovered in a single gcd iteration is at least $\varepsilon^2(n)/4$. The number of oracle queries in a single iteration is at most $(6n + 3) \cdot m = 2\varepsilon^{-2}(n) \cdot (6n + 3) \cdot \log_e 26n$. The expected running time to invert x is dominated by the number of oracle queries. Thus it is bounded above by $8\varepsilon^{-4}(n) \cdot (6n+3) \cdot \log_e 26n = \Theta\left(\varepsilon^{-4}(n) \cdot n \log n\right)$. Substituting $\varepsilon(n) = 1/poly(n)$, the overall run time is polynomial in n.

To summerize, we have demonstrated a probabilistic polynomial-time inversion algorithm for RSA using any $\frac{1}{4} + \frac{1}{poly(n)}$ oracle $\mathcal{O}_\mathcal{L}$. In other words

Theorem 4.4.1: *RSA least significant bit is $\frac{1}{4} + \frac{1}{poly(n)}$ secure.*

CHAPTER 5

THE LEAST SIGNIFICANT BIT IS $\frac{1}{poly(n)}$ SECURE

We start this chapter by discussing the phenomena of error doubling which restricted the usefulness of the parity subroutine to $\frac{1}{4} + \frac{1}{poly(n)}$ oracles. We briefly describe the attempts to overcome this restriction by Vazirani and Vazirani [47], and by Goldreich [23]. We then sketch the very important idea of Schnorr and Alexi [43]. With their method as a new starting point, we introduce the notion of two points based sampling. This proves to be a strong enough tool to yield the desired $\frac{1}{poly(n)}$ security result.

5.1 Error Doubling and Attempts to Overcome it

The main source of errors in the parity subroutine is the errors of the oracle. A dx-measurement may be wrong if the oracle errs on either $[rx]_N$ or $[rx + dx]_N$. Thus the error probability of a dx-measurement might be twice the error probability of the oracle. It is indeed possible to construct an oracle whose error probability is $\frac{1}{4}$, such that when it is used by the parity subroutine, it will cause an error in each dx measurement with probability $\frac{1}{2}$.

Vazirani and Vazirani suggested that the way to overcome the error doubling phenomena in the dx measurement is by using the information supplied by $\mathcal{O}_\mathcal{L}$ more carefully. They used the fact that a dx measurement is correct not only if the oracle answers correctly on both queries, but also if $\mathcal{O}_\mathcal{L}$ is *wrong* on both. To determine the parity of dx they performed not only dx measurements, but also measurements of other quantities, whose relation to dx is known. Incorporating their new oracle sampling technique into the gcd inversion, they proved better than $\frac{1}{4}$ security result. Their analysis gave a 0.232 security result for the least significant bit. Goldreich used better combinatorial analysis to show that the Vazirani and Vazirani algorithm actually yields a 0.225 result.

On the other hand, Goldreich also pointed out some limitations of the Vazirani and Vazirani and similar proof techniques. In particular, he showed that such techniques could at best yield $\frac{1}{6}$ security result – still a long way from the desired $\frac{1}{poly(n)}$ security.

5.2 Schnorr and Alexi Improvement

Schnorr and Alexi suggested the following brilliant idea to overcome error doubling: Instead of querying the oracle for the least significant bit of both points, query the oracle only for the least significant bit of one point. The least significant bit of the other point should be known beforehand. This way the oracle is queried only about one point in each measurement and the error is caused by single position queries rather than by pairs of positions. This enables the error probability per a single measurement to be approximately the oracle's error, rather than twice this quantity as before.

Schnorr and Alexi [43] implementation of this idea is based on trying all possibilities for the least significant bit of $L = \theta(\log n)$ random, mutually independent positions $w_i = r_i x$. These L positions are used as "end points" when trying to determine the parity of dx in all $O(n)$ dx-measurements of the gcd algorithm. Using the fact that the L positions are independent, Chernoff bound implies that the error probability in deciding the parity of dx by the majority of L dx-measurements is $2^{-\Omega(L\varepsilon^2)} < \frac{1}{12n+6}$ (here ε is a constant). This guarantees that the accumulated error probability in deciding the parity of all $6n + 3$ dx's in the modified binary gcd algorithm is $< \frac{1}{2}$, small enough to put the algorithm in random polynomial time.

Note that the running time of Schnorr and Alexi's algorithm is exponential in L. On the other hand, the probabilistic analysis requires that $L = \Omega(\log n/\varepsilon^2)$. Thus, ε can not be replaced by any function of N which tends to 0 with $N \to \infty$.

5.3 Two Points Based Sampling

In this section, we introduce a new method for generating many points (multiples of x) with known least-significant bits. These points are generated in a way which guarantees that they are "random" enough to be used as a good sample of the oracle. Specifically, these points will be generated such that the following properties hold:

1) Each point is uniformly distributed in Z_N.

2) The points are pairwise independent.

3) The least significant bit of each point is known.

The m points $[r_i x]_N$ are generated by picking two random independent elements $k, l \in Z_N$ with uniform distribution, and computing $[r_i x]_N = [(k + il)x]_N$, for $1 \leq i \leq m$. Define the random variables $y, z \in Z_N$ by $y = [kx]_N$, $z = [lx]_N$. The least-significant bits of the $[r_i x]_N$'s are found as follows: We try all possibilities for the least-significant bit of y, z, and for their approximate magnitude in one of the intervals $\left[i\frac{N}{m^{1.5}}, (i+1)\frac{N}{m^{1.5}}\right)$, where $0 \leq i < m^{1.5}$ (see figure 5.1).

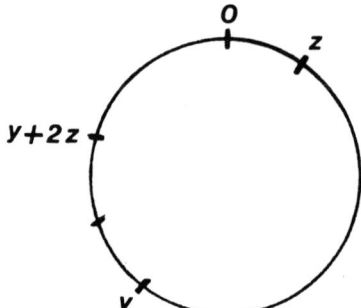

Fig. 5.1 – The points y, z and $y + 2z$

There are $(2 \cdot m^{1.5})^2 = 4m^3$ possibilities altogether, and exactly one of them is correct. Let us now assume that we are dealing with the correct choice, i.e. both least-significant bit and approximate magnitude of y, z are known. Since the location of both y and z are known up to $\frac{N}{m^{1.5}}$, the integer $w_i = y + iz$ is known up to $\frac{N}{m^{1.5}} + \frac{iN}{m^{1.5}} < \frac{2N}{m^{0.5}}$ ($1 \le i \le m$). Notice that $[w_i]_N$ is a random element in Z_N with uniform probability distribution. Therefore, the probability that the integer w_i falls in an interval of length $\frac{2N}{m^{0.5}}$ containing an integral multiple of N is exactly $\frac{2}{m^{0.5}}$. If w_i is not in such an interval, then the integral quotient of $\frac{w_i}{N}$ is determined by i and the approximate locations of y and z. This in turn, together with the least-significant bits of y and z, determines the least significant bit of $[w_i]_N = [r_i x]_N$.

The generation of $[r_i x]_N$'s is performed once per each gcd invocation, as part of step 1 (the randomization step) in the inversion procedure of section 4.3. The choice of k and l ($y = [kx]_N$, $z = [lx]_N$) is independent of the choice of a, b.

The original parity subroutine makes use of random independent r_i's, and queries the oracle for the least-significant bits of $[r_i x]$ and $[r_i x + dx]_N$. We modify it by using the $r_i x$'s generated above, and querying the oracle only for the least significant bit of $[r_i x + dx]_N$. The least significant bit of $[r_i x]_N$ is known beforehand (with very high probability).

5.4 Probability Analysis

In this section we analyze the success probability of the inversion algorithm. We show that given $\mathcal{O}_\mathcal{L}$, an $\varepsilon(n) = \frac{1}{poly(n)}$ oracle for RSA least-significant bit, the inversion algorithm is in random polynomial-time.

Consider one run of the gcd procedure. Let us modify again the definition of "small', and say that h is small if $abs_N(h) < \frac{N\varepsilon(n)}{2}$. Suppose that $[ax]_N$ and $[bx]_N$ are both small and are relatively prime. This happens with probability $\varepsilon(n)^2 \cdot \frac{6}{\pi^2}$. Recall that a gcd run consists of at most $6n+3$ calls to the parity subroutine. Then the run is successful (yields x) if all calls to the parity subroutine return correct answers.

From this point on, probabilities are taken over all choices of y, z with uniform probability distribution (x and d are fixed). There is a certain probability that the parity subroutine will err. We will bound this error probability from above, so that even when multiplied by $6n + 3$ it is still small ($< \frac{1}{2}$). Recall that on input d the parity subroutine conducts m dx-measurements. Each measurement "supports" either $par_N(dx) = 0$ or $par_N(dx) = 1$. The subroutine returns the majority decision.

For every $1 \leq i \leq m$, the i-th individual dx-measurement consists of comparing the precomputed least significant bit of $[r_i x]_N$ to the answer of the oracle for the least significant bit of $[r_i x + dx]_N$. Such measurement has three potential sources of error:

1) The oracle errs on the least significant bit of $[r_i x + dx]_N$.
2) There is a wraparound 0 when $[dx]_N$ is added to $[r_i x]_N$.
3) The precomputed least significant bit of $[r_i x]_N$ is wrong. This may happen only if $abs_N(r_i x) < \frac{2N}{m^{0.5}}$.

Note that $[r_i x + dx]_N$ is uniformly distributed in Z_N. Therefore type 1 error has probability $\frac{1}{2} - \varepsilon(n)$. Since $abs_N(dx) < \frac{\varepsilon(n) N}{2}$, type 2 error has probability at most $\frac{\varepsilon(n)}{2}$. Type 3 error has probability at most $\frac{2}{m^{0.5}}$. For $m > \left(\frac{8}{\varepsilon(n)}\right)^2$, the overall error probability is bounded above by $\frac{1}{2} - \frac{\varepsilon(n)}{4}$.

Define the random variable

$$\varsigma_i = \begin{cases} 1 & \text{if the } i\text{-th } dx\text{-measurement is wrong} \\ 0 & \text{if the } i\text{-th } dx\text{-measurement is correct} \end{cases}$$

Clearly, $Exp(\varsigma_i) = Pr(\varsigma_i = 1) < \frac{1}{2} - \frac{\varepsilon(n)}{4}$ and

$$Var(\varsigma_i) = Exp(\varsigma_i^2) - Exp^2(\varsigma_i)$$
$$= Exp(\varsigma_i) - Exp^2(\varsigma_i)$$
$$= Exp(\varsigma_i)(1 - Exp(\varsigma_i)) < \frac{1}{4}$$

Since $Exp(\varsigma_i) < \frac{1}{2} - \frac{\varepsilon(n)}{4}$, we have

$$Pr\left(\frac{1}{m}\sum_{i=1}^{m}\varsigma_i \geq \frac{1}{2}\right) \leq Pr\left(\left|\frac{1}{m}\sum_{i=1}^{m}\varsigma_i - Exp(\varsigma_i)\right| \geq \frac{\varepsilon(n)}{4}\right)$$

By Chebyshev's inequality [21, p. 219]

$$Pr\left(\left|\frac{1}{m}\sum_{i=1}^{m}\varsigma_i - Exp(\varsigma_i)\right| \geq \frac{\varepsilon(n)}{4}\right) \leq \frac{Var(\frac{1}{m}\sum_{i=1}^{m}\varsigma_i)}{(\varepsilon(n)/4)^2} \quad (*)$$

In order to bound the variance, we will now show that the ς_i are pairwise independent. First, we prove that if $i \neq j$ then $[r_i x]_N$ and $[r_j x]_N$ are two independent random variables ($1 \leq i,j \leq m$). This follows from the fact that $i - j$ has a multiplicative inverse modulo N, and so for every $c_1, c_2 \in Z_N$, the equations

$$y + iz \equiv c_1 \pmod{N}$$
$$y + jz \equiv c_2 \pmod{N}$$

have a unique solution in terms of $y, z \in Z_N$. Thus, for every $c_1, c_2 \in Z_N$,

$$Pr([r_i x]_N = c_1 \text{ and } [r_j x]_N = c_2) = \frac{1}{N^2}$$
$$= Pr([r_i x]_N = c_1) \cdot Pr([r_j x]_N = c_2) .$$

Since ς_i is a function of $r_i x$, we conclude that ς_i and ς_j are also independent random variables with identical distribution. (Whenever the same function is applied to two independent random variables, the two results are independent random variables.) Let $\overline{\varsigma_i} = \varsigma_i - Exp(\varsigma_i)$. By pairwise independence $Exp(\overline{\varsigma_i} \cdot \overline{\varsigma_j}) = Exp(\overline{\varsigma_i}) \cdot Exp(\overline{\varsigma_j})$. Hence,

$$Var\left(\frac{1}{m}\sum_{i=1}^{m}\varsigma_i\right) = \frac{1}{m^2}\sum_{i=1}^{m}\sum_{j=1}^{m}Exp\left(\overline{\varsigma_i} \cdot \overline{\varsigma_j}\right)$$
$$= \frac{1}{m^2}\left(\sum_{i=1}^{m}Exp\left(\overline{\varsigma_i}^2\right) + \sum_{1 \leq i \neq j \leq m}Exp\left(\overline{\varsigma_i}\right)Exp\left(\overline{\varsigma_j}\right)\right)$$
$$= \frac{1}{m^2} \cdot m \cdot Exp\left(\overline{\varsigma_1}^2\right)$$
$$< \frac{1}{4m}$$

Substituting this bound in $(*)$, we get $Pr\left(\frac{1}{m}\sum_{i=1}^{m}\varsigma_i \geq \frac{1}{2}\right) < \frac{4}{m\varepsilon^2(n)}$.

Finally, we analyze the expected running time to invert with an $\varepsilon(n)$-oracle. The parity subroutine is invoked by the gcd at most $6n + 3$ times. Assume that $[ax]_N$ and $[bx]_N$ are small, and that the locations of y, z and their least significant bits are correctly known. Under these conditions, the error probability for the gcd is bounded above by

$$(6n + 3) \cdot Pr(\text{ error for a single parity call }) < (6n + 3) \cdot \frac{4}{m\varepsilon^2(n)}$$

Substituting $m = 8\varepsilon^{-2}(n) \cdot (6n + 3)$, the error probability for one binary gcd is bounded above by $\frac{1}{2}$. For this value of m, the running time of the *gcd* procedure is $O(m \cdot n) = O(\varepsilon^{-2}(n) \cdot n^2)$. To satisfy the condition on y and z, we run $O(m^3)$ copies of the gcd procedure, so the running time per choice of a and b is $O(m^4 \cdot n)$. The expected number of a, b pairs we have to try is $O(\varepsilon^{-2}(n))$, so that overall, the expected running time of the inverting algorithm is

$$O(\varepsilon^{-2}(n) m^4 n) = O(\varepsilon^{-10}(n) n^5) \ .$$

For $\varepsilon(n) = \frac{1}{poly(n)}$ we can thus recover the original message in random polynomial time, as desired. This implies

Theorem 5.4.1: *RSA least-significant bit is $\frac{1}{poly(n)}$-secure.*

CHAPTER 6

EXTENSIONS AND APPLICATIONS

In the first section of this chapter we extend the bit security result to simultaneous security of $\log n$ least-significant bits. The second section deals with an extension in a different direction – secure bits for Rabin's encryption function (squaring modulo a composite number). Yet another direction is explored in the third section – bit security for RSA over multi-prime composites, with known partial factorization. We conclude with applications of the bit security results to Blum–Micali type pseudo random bits generators to and to Goldwasser–Micali type probabilistic encryptions. In particular, we show that Rabin/RSA encryption can be *directly* applied in both cases, without using Yao's exclusive-or technique [50].

6.1 Simultaneous Security

Definition 6.1.1: *We say that the j least-significant bits are simultaneously secure if inverting E_N is polynomial-time reducible to distinguishing, given $E_N(x)$, between the string of j least-significant bits of x and a randomly selected j-bit string.*

We defined the notion of simultaneous security in terms of an indistinguishability test. It is also possible to define simultaneous security in terms of an unpredictability test: Given $E_N(x)$ and the $j-1$ least-significant bits of x, the j-th least significant bit of x is still $\frac{1}{poly(n)}$ secure.

Yao [50] has shown that the indistinguishability test is equivalent to the unpredictability test. It turns out that our proof technique easily extends to show that $\log n$ least-significant bits pass the unpredictability test. By Yao's result, this implies simultaneous security for the $\log n$ RSA least-significant bits.

Theorem 6.1.2: Let $j = O(\log n)$.

a) The j-th least significant bit in the binary expansion of the plaintext is $\frac{1}{poly(n)}$ secure.

b) The j least-significant bits of the plaintext are simultaneously secure.

Proof.

a) First note that in the two point based sampling, it is possible to guess not only the 1-st least-significant bit of y and z, but all j least-significant bits of y and z. The overhead for trying all possibilities is 2^j, which is polynomial in n. Together with the locations of y and z, these bits will determine all j least-significant bits of each $[r_i x]_N$. Similarly, we can assume that the gcd of $[ax]_N$ and $[bx]_N$ is 2^{j-1} (instead of 1). This way all $[dx]_N$'s in the gcd calculation will have zeros in all $j-1$ least-significant bits. Finally, we replace all references to the least-significant bit in the inverting algorithm, by references to the j-th least-significant bit. This can be done since we now have access to an oracle for the j-th least-significant bit.

(This method of transforming certain inverting algorithms which use an oracle for the 1-st least significant bit into inverting algorithms which use an oracle for the j-th least significant bit originates from Vazirani and Vazirani [47].)

b) Going through the proof of part (a), notice that when querying the oracle about the j-th least significant bit of $[r_i x + dx]_N$ we can give it the $j-1$ previous bits of $[r_i x + dx]_N$. This is the case since if no wraparound occurs, these $j-1$ bits are the same as the $j-1$ least-significant bits of $[r_i x]_N$, which we know. Therefore the j bit of x is unpredictable, given the previous $j-1$ bits and $E_N(x)$. Using Yao's theorem, the proof is complete. □

Remark: Vazirani and Vazirani [48] had previously shown that certain inverting algorithms which use a $\varepsilon(n)$-oracle for RSA least-significant bit, can be transformed into inverting algorithms which use a $\varepsilon(n)$-oracle for predicting x_j (given $x_{j-1}, \ldots, x_1$). It turns out that the inverting algorithm of chapter 5 falls into the above category; this yields an alternative (but much harder) way of proving Theorem 6.1.2(b).

6.2 Secure Bits in Rabin's Encryption Function

The Rabin encryption function is operating on the message space Z_N, where $N = pq$ is the product of two large primes (which are kept secret). The encryption of x is $E_N(x) = [x^2]_N$. The ciphertext space is $Q_N = \{y|\ \exists x\ y \equiv x^2 \pmod{N}\}$. Rabin [39] has shown that extracting square roots ("inverting E_N") is polynomially equivalent to factoring N.

The function E_N defined above is four-to-one rather than being one-to-one (as is the case in the RSA). Blum [4] has pointed out the cryptographic importance of the fact that for $p \equiv q \equiv 3 \pmod{4}$, E_N induces a permutation over Q_N. Composite numbers of this form will be called *Blum integers*.

Goldwasser, Micali and Tong [26] have presented a predicate whose evaluation is as hard as factoring. Specifically, they showed that if $p \equiv 3 \pmod{4}$ and $p \equiv q \pmod{8}$ then factoring N is polynomially reducible to guessing their predicate with success probability $1 - \frac{1}{n}$.

Using the techniques of chapter 5, we show that the least significant bit in a variant of Rabin's encryption function is also $\frac{1}{poly(n)}$ secure. Our proof uses only elementary number theory, and holds for all Blum integers.

Throughout this section we make use of the *Jacobi symbol*. Let us review the definition and some properties of the Jacobi symbol (for further details, see [36, ch. 3]). Let p be an odd prime number, and h an integer relatively prime to p. The *Legendre symbol* $\left(\frac{h}{p}\right)$ is defined to be 1 if h is a quadratic residue modulo p, and -1 otherwise. For $N = pq$, a product of two odd primes, and h relatively prime to N, the *Jacobi symbol* $\left(\frac{h}{N}\right)$ is defined to be $\left(\frac{h}{p}\right) \cdot \left(\frac{h}{q}\right)$. Even though the definition of the Jacobi symbol uses the factorization of N, it can be easily computed even if N's factorization is not given. Another fact which is used in this section is that $\left(\frac{h \cdot h'}{N}\right) = \left(\frac{h}{N}\right) \cdot \left(\frac{h'}{N}\right)$.

Let N be a Blum integer. Define

$$S_N \stackrel{def}{=} \left\{x\ |\ 0 \leq x < \frac{N}{2}\right\}$$

$$M_N \stackrel{def}{=} \left\{x\ |\ 0 \leq x < \frac{N}{2} \wedge \left(\frac{x}{N}\right) = 1\right\}.$$

Redefine E_N for $x \in M_N$ as

$$E_N(x) = \begin{cases} [x^2]_N, & \text{if } [x^2]_N < \frac{N}{2}; \\ [N - x^2]_N, & \text{otherwise.} \end{cases}$$

This makes E_N a $1-1$ mapping from M_N onto itself. The intractability result of Rabin still holds. That is, factoring N is polynomially reducible to inverting E_N. Let $L_N(x)$ denote the least-significant bit of x.

We'd like to show that given $\mathcal{O}_\mathcal{L}$, an $\varepsilon(n) = \frac{1}{poly(n)}$ oracle for E_N least-significant bit, we can invert E_N (and thus factor N) in random polynomial-time. The basic idea in the reduction is similar to the RSA case. Given $E_N(x)$, map x at random by computing $E_N(ax), E_N(bx)$, and try to retrieve $\gcd([ax]_N, [bx]_N)$. To do that, we pick m random, pairwise independent points $[r_i x]_N$ which are uniformly distributed in S_N, such that their least-significant bits are known. We want to determine the parity of $[dx]_N$ for small $[dx]_N \in Z_N$ (not necessarily in M_N or even S_N). To this end, we would have liked to query the oracle for the least significant bit of $[r_i x + dx]_N$, as in the RSA case. However, if $[r_i x + dx]_N \notin M_N$, the oracle's answer does not correspond to $[r_i x + dx]_N$ (but rather to the square root of $[(r_i x + dx)^2]_N$ which resides in M_N). This ($[r_i x + dx]_N \notin M_N$) may happen if either $[r_i x + dx]_N \notin S_N$ or $\left(\frac{r_i x + dx}{N}\right) = -1$. The first case occurs with very low probability (since $[dx]_N$ is small and $[r_i x]_N$ is uniformly distributed in S_N). In the second case, which is easy to detect, we do not query the oracle, but flip a coin instead.

More formally, given the original encryption $E_N(x)$, pick $y = kx$ and $z = lx$, two random multiples of x. By exhausting all possibilities, the approximate magnitude in Z_N of y and z, and their least-significant bits are known. Let $v_i = [y + iz]_N, 1 \leq i \leq m$. Define

$$w_i = \begin{cases} v_i, & \text{if } v_i < \frac{N}{2}; \\ N - v_i, & \text{otherwise.} \end{cases}$$

We have $w_i = [r_i x]_N$, where r_i is either $k + il$ or $-(k + il)$. If $w_i = [r_i x]_N$ is not in a $\frac{2N}{m^{0.5}}$ interval around 0 or $\frac{N}{2}$, then we can determine which of the two alternatives for r_i holds, and can compute the least significant bit of w_i. Therefore we get

$$Pr(\text{ least-significant bit of } w_i \text{ is unknown}) \leq \frac{4}{m^{0.5}}.$$

It will be convenient to slightly change the definition of "small" here. In this section h is small means $abs_N(h) < \frac{N\varepsilon(n)}{8}$ (instead of $abs_N(h) < \frac{N\varepsilon(n)}{2}$ as in chapter 5). This will restrict all $[dx]_N$'s in the gcd calculation to be small. Doing this, the probability that a wraparound either 0 or $\frac{N}{2}$ occurs when $[dx]_N$ is added to $[r_i x]_N$ is no greater than $\frac{\varepsilon(n)}{4}$.

The remaining step is to determine the parity of $[dx]_N$ by comparing the known least-significant bit of $[r_i x]_N$ with the least-significant bit of $[r_i x + dx]_N$. If $\left(\frac{r_i+d}{N}\right) = 1$, we feed the oracle $\mathcal{O}_\mathcal{L}$ with $E_N(r_i x + dx)$, and take its answer as our guess for the least significant bit of $[r_i x + dx]_N$. If, on the other hand, $\left(\frac{r_i+d}{N}\right) = -1$, we use the outcome of a coin flip as our guess for the least significant bit of $[r_i x + dx]_N$. To analyze this procedure, notice first that the number of elements in S_N with Jacobi symbol 1 equals the number of elements in S_N with Jacobi symbol -1 (since these are equal in Z_N, -1 has Jacobi symbol 1, and $Z_N = S_N \bigcup -1 \cdot S_N$). As $[r_i x + dx]_N$ is (almost) uniformly distributed in S_N, the probability that $\left(\frac{r_i+d}{N}\right) = 1$ is (almost) $1/2$. In this case, $[r_i x + dx]_N \in M_N$, so that $\mathcal{O}_\mathcal{L}$ guess for $L_N(r_i x + dx)$ is correct with probability $\geq \frac{1}{2} + \varepsilon(n)$. Otherwise, our guess is correct with probability exactly $1/2$. Averaging over the two cases, our guess is correct with probability (almost exactly) $\frac{1}{2} + \frac{\varepsilon(n)}{2}$. Accounting for all the error terms, the above procedure makes the correct guess for the least significant bit of $[r_i x + dx]_N$ with probability at least

$$\frac{1}{2} + \frac{\varepsilon(n)}{2} - \frac{4}{m^{0.5}} - \frac{\varepsilon(n)}{4} > \frac{1}{2} + \frac{\varepsilon(n)}{8}.$$

The rest of the analysis is similar to the analysis presented in chapter 5. This implies

Theorem 6.2.1: The least-significant bit for the modified Rabin encryption function is $\frac{1}{poly(n)}$-secure. That is, inverting $E_N(\cdot)$ is probabilistic polynomial-time reducible to the following: Given $E_N(x)$ (for $x \in M_N$), guess the least significant bit of x with success probability $\frac{1}{2} + \frac{1}{poly(n)}$.

Corollary 6.2.2: Factoring a Blum integer, N, is polynomially reducible to guessing $L_N(x)$ with success probability $\frac{1}{2} + \frac{1}{poly(n)}$ when given $E_N(x)$, for $x \in M_N$.

The proofs from the previous chapter about simultaneous security of $\log n$ least significant bits hold here just as well.

6.3 Multi-Prime Moduli with Partial Factorization

The results about bit security for the RSA function were described with respect to composite numbers N which are the product of two large primes. However, the same proofs hold for the case of multi-prime composite $N = p_1 p_2 \ldots p_k$, where the exponent e is relatively prime to $\varphi(N)$.

It is more surprising that bit security holds *even if partial factorization of N is known*. In fact, the least-significant bit is secure even if all but one pair of primes are known. That means that we can reduce the problem inverting E_M ($M = p_1 p_2$) to the bit security of E_N ($N = p_1 p_2 p_3 \ldots p_k$), where all primes but p_1, p_2 are known. More formally

Theorem 6.3.1: Let $N = p_1 p_2 p_3 \ldots p_k$, $M = p_1 p_2$, and $n = \log_2 N$ be the length of N. Let e be relatively prime to $\varphi(N)$, $E_M(x) = x^e \pmod{M}$, and $E_N(x) = x^e \pmod{N}$. Then the following three tasks are computationally equivalent, (each is $poly(n)$ time reducible to the other).

1) Invert E_M.

2) Invert E_N.

3) Given $M, p_3, p_4, \ldots, p_l$ (a partial factorization of $N = M p_3 p_4 \cdots p_l$) and $E_N(z) \in Z_N$, guess $L_N(z)$ with success probability exceeding $\frac{1}{2} + \frac{1}{poly(n)}$.

Proof. The hard part, the equivalence of (2) and (3) is proved in exactly the same way as theorem 5.4.1. To show that (1) is reducible to (2) we use the Chinese remainder theorem [36, p. 30]. Given $a = E_M(x) \in Z_M$, we first find $b = E_N(z) \in Z_N$ so that $z \in Z_N$ and $E_N(z) \equiv E_M(x) \pmod{M}$. To do that, find a number $0 \leq b < N$ which satisfies $b \equiv a \pmod{M}$ and $b \equiv 1 \pmod{N/M}$. With an oracle for (2), $z = E_N^{-1}(b)$ can be recovered. But $x^e \equiv z^e \pmod{M}$ implies $x \equiv z \pmod{M}$. Thus $x \bmod M$ is the desired answer. Similarly, (2) is reducible to (1) using the partial factorization of N. (In fact, only this last reduction requires the partial factorization.) □

The bit security of RSA for multi-prime composites with known partial factorization was used in the cryptographic protocol of [16] for verifiable secret sharing. A more complicated argument holds for bit security of Rabin's function under similar circumstances, as was recently shown in [15].

6.4 Direct Construction of Pseudo-Random Bit Generators

A pseudo-random bit generator is a device which "expands randomness." Given a truly random bit string s (the seed), it expands it to a longer pseudo-random sequence. The question of "how random" this pseudo-random sequence is, depends on the definition of randomness we use. A strong requirement is indistinguishability – the expanded sequence will pass all polynomial time statistical tests. Namely, given a pseudo-random and a truly random sequences of equal length, no probabilistic polynomial time algorithm can tell which is which with success probability significantly greater than $\frac{1}{2}$ (as we've mentioned in section 1, Yao [50] showed that this requirement is equivalent to the unpredictability of the next bit).

Blum and Micali [7] presented a general scheme for constructing such *strong pseudo-random* generators. Let $g : M \to M$ be a $1-1$ one-way function, and $B(x)$ be a $\frac{1}{poly(\log |M|)}$ secure predicate for g. Starting with a random $s \in M$, the sequence obtained by iterating g and outputting $b_i = B\left(g^i(s)\right)$ for each iteration is strongly pseudo-random. Using their $\frac{1}{poly(\log p)}$ security result for the $half_p$ bit in discrete exponentiation modulo a prime p, Blum and Micali gave a concrete implementation of the scheme, based on the intractability assumption of computing discrete logarithm. More generally, if $B_1(x), \ldots, B_k(x)$ are simultaneously secure bits for g, then the sequence obtained by iterating g

and outputting the string $\langle b_i^1 \ldots b_i^k \rangle = \langle B_1(g^i(s)) \ldots B_k(g^i(s)) \rangle$ for each iteration, is strongly pseudo-random. Long and Wigderson [33] have shown that the discrete exponentiation function has $\log \log p$ simultaneous secure bits. Their result implies that the Blum–Micali generator can be used to produces $\log \log p$ pseudo-random bits per each iteration of the discrete exponentiation.

Using our results, we get an efficient implementation of strong pseudo-random generators, based on the intractability assumption of inverting RSA/factoring. For the RSA case, the random seed $s \in Z_N$ is raised to the power e at every iteration. In the i-th iteration the generator outputs the $\log n$ least significant bits of $s^{e^i} \mod N$. For the factoring case, the modified Rabin function E_N is iteratively applied to the random seed $s \in M_N$. In the i-th iteration, the generator outputs the $\log n$ least-significant bits of $E_N^i(s) = \pm s^{2^i} \mod N$. Thus it outputs $\log n$ pseudo-random bits at the cost of one squaring and one subtraction modulo N, and is substantially more efficient than the discrete exponentiation generator. Previous strong pseudo-random generators based on factoring ([26], [3], [47]) required the use of the exclusive-or construction of Yao [50] and were less efficient.

Another efficient pseudo-random generator was previously constructed by Blum, Blum and Shub [5]. Their generator outputs one pseudo-random bit per one modular squaring. Blum, Blum and Shub proved that their generator is a strong pseudo-random generator if the problem of deciding quadratic residuosity modulo a composite number is intractable. Using our techniques, Vazirani and Vazirani [48] have pointed out that the Blum, Blum and Shub generator is strong also with respect to the problem of factoring Blum integers.

6.5 Application to Probabilistic Encryption

A probabilistic encryption scheme is said to leak no partial information if the following holds: *Whatever is efficiently computable about the plaintext given the ciphertext, is also efficiently computable without the ciphertext* [25]. Goldwasser and Micali presented a general scheme for constructing public-key probabilistic encryption schemes which leak no partial information, using a "secure trap-door predicate". A *secure trap-door predicate* is a predicate which is easy to evaluate given some "trap-door" information, but infeasible to guess with the slightest advantage without the "trap-door" information. Goldwasser and Micali also gave a concrete implementation of their scheme, under the intractability assumption of deciding quadratic residuosity modulo a composite number. A drawback of their implementation is that it expands each plaintext bit into a ciphertext block (of length equal to that of the composite modulus), and thus its information rate is low.

Using our results, we get an implementation of a probabilistic public-key encryption scheme which leaks no partial information, based on the intractability assumption of inverting RSA/factoring. For example, we describe the factoring case. To encrypt 0, choose x at random among all numbers in M_N with least-significant bit 0, and send $E_N(x)$. To encrypt 1, choose x at random among all numbers in M_N with least-significant bit 1, and send $E_N(x)$. This implementation is more efficient that the one in Goldwasser [24] which is also based on factoring. However, our implementation still suffers from a large bandwidth expansion.

Recently, Blum and Goldwasser [6] used our result to introduce a new implementation of probabilistic encryption, equivalent to factoring, in which the plaintext is only expanded by an *additive factor* of n bits. Blum and Goldwasser's scheme is approximately as efficient as the deterministic RSA while provably leaking no partial information, provided that factoring is intractable.

Part II

A New Knapsack-Type Cryptosystem

CHAPTER 7

THE NEW CRYPTOSYSTEM

7.1 Background

After Diffie and Hellman introduced the idea of public-key cryptography by [20], a number of implementations have been proposed. Most of these implementations† can be put into two categories:

a) PKC based on hard number-theoretic problems (e.g. RSA [42], Rabin [39], Williams [49], Goldwasser–Micali [25]).

b) PKC related to the knapsack problem (e.g. Merkle–Hellman [35], Shamir [46], Brickell [10]).

While no efficient attacks against number theoretic PKC are known, several knapsack-type PKC have been shown to be insecure. Most of those systems have a concealed "superincreasing" sequence. Shamir made the first successful attack on the basic Merkle–Hellman system [45]. Following his attack, other attacks against more complicated systems were proposed. In particular, Brickell [12] found a way to break the general Merkle–Hellman scheme. A different attack is the "low density" attack of Lagarias and Odlyzko [31]. The most interesting point about this last attack is that it does not make any assumption about how the system was constructed, and thus might be applicable to any knapsack-type cryptosystem (unlike, say, Shamir's attack which relies heavily on the superincreasing underlying sequence). As a result of these attacks, knapsack-type PKC, which are either based on superincreasing sequences or have very low density, seem to be vulnerable.

---

† with the exception of the McEliece system [34], which is based on error correcting codes

Here we propose a new knapsack-type PKC which has high density and a completely different basis. The underlying construction makes use of a result due to Bose and Chowla [8] about unique representation of sums in "dense" finite sequences. To create the encryption-decryption keys in this construction, discrete logarithms in finite fields are to be computed. Once this is done, encryption is very fast (linear time) and decryption is reasonably fast (comparable to RSA). Hence creating the keys is the hard part. While there are no polynomial time algorithms known for taking discrete logarithms, there are practical algorithms (most notably the ones due to Pohlig and Hellman [38] and Coppersmith [18]) in some special cases. To demonstrate the feasibility of such cases, we have constructed a real life instance of our cryptosystem. The construction is over the finite field $GF(197^{24})$. We believe that a system of that size will foil both low-density and exhaustive search attacks. The running-time for constructing the system was a couple of hours on a minicomputer. This time consuming task is done only once by each user, so it is acceptable from a practical point of view.

We'd like to remark that all known number theoretic PKC are at most as hard as factoring and hence are all reducible to the problem of taking discrete logarithms in composite moduli (see appendix 1). Should this discrete logarithm problem become tractable (thus rendering all "number-theoretic" PKC insecure), our system will become easier to create for even larger size knapsacks.

7.2 Knapsack-Type Cryptosystems

The $0-1$ knapsack problem is the following NP-complete [22] decision problem: Given a set $A = \{\ a_i\ |\ 0 \leq i \leq n-1\}$ of non-negative integers and a non-negative integer S, is there an integer solution to $\sum x_i a_i = S$ where all x_i are 0 or 1? A different variant of the problem is to remove the $0-1$ restriction on the x_i (but insisting they remain non-negative integers) and bounding their total weight $\sum x_i \leq h$.

Knapsack-type public-key cryptosystems are based on the intractability of finding a solution to $S = \sum x_i a_i$ even when a solution is known to exist. In such systems, each user publishes a set A of a_i and a bound h. A plaintext message consisting of an integer vector $M = (x_0, x_1, \ldots, x_{n-1})$ with weight $\leq h$ is encrypted by setting

$$E(M) = \sum x_i a_i .$$

The knapsack elements a_i are chosen in such way that the equation is easily solved if certain secret *trapdoor* information is known. The exact nature of this information depends on the particular system in question. A general property of knapsack-type PKC is that encryption is easy – all you have to do is to add.

7.3 Bose-Chowla Theorem

In 1936, Sidon raised the question of whether there exist "dense" sequences whose h-fold sums are unique. *Given n and h, non-negative integers, is there a sequence $A = \{a_i \,|\, 0 \leq i \leq n-1\}$ of non-negative integers, such that all sums of exactly h elements (repetitions allowed) out of A are distinct?* It is easy to construct such sequences if the a_i are growing exponentially in n: For example, the sequence $\{1, h, h^2, \ldots, h^{n-1}\}$ has the above property (but does not work even for $h+1$ element sums, since $h^2 + h \cdot 1 = (h+1) \cdot h$). But can one construct such sequence with the a_i growing only polynomially fast in n? Bose and Chowla [8] found a very elegant way of constructing such sequences with $1 \leq a_i \leq n^h - 1$ for all $0 \leq i \leq n-1$. (See Halberstram and Roth [27,ch.2] for an overview of the subject.) Here, we'll present a slightly modified version of Bose-Chowla theorem, which will fit well with our cryptographic application.

Bose-Chowla Theorem: *Let p be a prime, $h \geq 2$ an integer. Then there exists a sequence $A = \{a_i \,|\, 0 \leq i \leq p-1\}$ of integers such that*

1. $1 \leq a_i \leq p^h - 1 \quad (i = 0, 1, \ldots, p-1)$.

2. *If $(x_0, x_1, \ldots x_{p-1})$ and $(y_0, y_1, \ldots y_{p-1})$ are two distinct vectors with non-negative integral coordinates and $\sum_{i=0}^{p-1} x_i, \sum_{i=0}^{p-1} y_i \leq h$, then $\sum_{i=0}^{p-1} x_i a_i \neq \sum_{i=0}^{p-1} y_i a_i$.*

Proof. The construction takes place in the finite field $GF(p)$ and in its h-degree extension, $GF(p^h)$. Let $t \in GF(p^h)$ be algebraic of degree h over $GF(p)$ (i.e. the minimal polynomial in $GF(p)[x]$ having t as its root is of degree h). Let g

be a multiplicative generator (primitive element) of $GF(p^h)$ (that is $GF(p^h)^* = \{g^e \mid 0 \leq e \leq p^h - 1\}$). Look at an additive shift by t of the base field, $GF(p)$, namely at the set

$$t + GF(p) = \{t + i \mid i = 0, 1, \ldots, p - 1\} \subset GF(p^h) \ .$$

Let $a_i = \log_g(t + i)$ $(i = 0, 1 \ldots, p - 1)$ the logarithm of $t + i$ to the base g in $GF(p^h)$. Then the a_i are all integers in the interval $[1, p^h - 1]$ and they satisfy the distinctness of h-fold sums: For suppose there are two vectors $\vec{x}$, $\vec{y}$ of non-negative integers satisfying $(*)$, $(**)$, and $(***)$.

$$(x_0, x_1, \ldots x_{p-1}) \neq (y_0, y_1, \ldots y_{p-1}) \tag{$*$}$$

$$\sum_{i=0}^{p-1} x_i, \sum_{i=0}^{p-1} y_i \leq h \tag{$**$}$$

$$\sum_{i=0}^{p-1} x_i a_i = \sum_{i=0}^{p-1} y_i a_i \tag{$***$}$$

Then the following equality holds in $GF(p^h)$

$$g^{\sum_{i=0}^{p-1} x_i a_i} = g^{\sum_{i=0}^{p-1} y_i a_i}$$

and so

$$\prod_{i=0}^{p-1} (g^{a_i})^{x_i} = \prod_{i=0}^{p-1} (g^{a_i})^{y_i} \ .$$

Using the equality $g^{a_i} = t + i$, and considering only the non-zero x_i, y_i, we get

$$(t + k_1)^{x_1}(t + k_2)^{x_2} \ldots (t + k_l)^{x_l} = (t + j_1)^{y_1}(t + j_2)^{y_2} \ldots (t + j_k)^{y_k} \ ,$$

where $\{k_1, k_2, \ldots, k_l\}$ and $\{j_1, j_2, \ldots, j_k\}$ are two different non-empty subsets of $\{0, 1, \ldots, p - 1\}$, with at most h elements each. Both sides of the last equation are thus distinct *monic* polynomials of degree $\leq h$ with coefficients in $GF(p)$, so by subtracting them we get:

t is a root of a non-zero polynomial, with coefficients in $GF(p)$, of degree $\leq h - 1$.

This contradicts the fact that t is algebraic of degree h over $GF(p)$. □

Remarks:

1. From the above proof it is clear that ℓ sums ($\ell \leq h$) of A are distinct not only over Z, but also modulo $p^h - 1$.

2. The requirement "p is a prime" can be replaced by "p is a prime power" with no change in the claim or its proof.

7.4 How the Cryptosystem is Constructed and Used

In this section we describe how the new cryptosystem is created and used. We start with an informal (and slightly simplified) description. Next, a step-by-step recipe for generating the cryptosystem, encrypting messages and decrypting ciphertexts is given.

The first step is to pick a prime (or a prime power) p and h such that $GF(p^h)$ is amenable for discrete logarithm computations. We leave p and h as unspecified parameters in this section, and elaborate more on their exact choice in section 7 (the approximate magnitudes will be $p \approx 200$, $h \approx 25$). Once p and h are chosen, we pick $t \in GF(p^h)$ of algebraic degree h over the base field, and a primitive element $g \in GF(p^h)$ (both t and g are picked at random from the many possible candidates). Following Bose and Chowla, logarithms (to base g) of the p elements in $GF(p) + t$ are computed. These p integers are then scrambled, using a randomly chosen permutation. The scrambled integers are published. Together with p and h, they constitute the public encryption key, while the elements t, g and the unscrambling permutation constitute the secret decryption key. In order to encrypt a binary message of length p and weight h, a user adds the knapsack elements with 1 in the corresponding message location, and sends the sum. (Section 6 deals with the question of transforming "regular", unconstrained binary strings to those of the above form.) When the legitimate receiver gets a sum, he first raises the generator g to it, and expresses the result as a degree h polynomial in t over $GF(p)$. The h roots of this polynomial are found by successive substitutions. Applying the inverse of the original permutation, the indices of the plaintext having the bit 1 are recovered.

a. System Generation

1. Let p be a prime power, $h \leq p$ an integer such that discrete logarithms in $GF(p^h)$ can be efficiently computed.

2. Pick a random $t \in GF(p^h)$ that is algebraic of degree h over $GF(p)$. This will be done by finding $f(t)$, a random irreducible monic polynomial of degree h in $GF(p)[t]$, and representing $GF(p^h)$ arithmetic by $GF(p)[t]/<f(t)>$. (That is, elements of $GF(p^h)$ are polynomials of degree $\leq h-1$ with coefficients in $GF(p)$, and addition/multiplication operations are done modulo p and $f(t)$.)

3. Pick $g \in GF(p^h)$, g a multiplicative generator of $GF(p^h)$ *at random*. This will be done by picking a random $r \in GF(p^h)$ until one which satisfies $r^{(p^h-1)/s} \neq 1$ (for all prime factors s of $p^h - 1$) is found. It should be noted that in our system, $p^h - 1$ will have only *small* prime divisors, and so it is easy to verify that a given r passes the above test. Since the density of such generators is relatively high in all cases (regardless of any special properties of p and h), the above procedure is indeed feasible.

4. Construction following Bose-Chowla theorem: Compute $a_i = \log_g(t+i)$ for $i = 0, 1, 2, \ldots, p-1$.

5. Scramble the a_i's: Let $\pi : \{0, 1, \ldots, p-1\} \to \{0, 1, \ldots, p-1\}$ be a randomly chosen permutation. Set $b_i = a_{\pi(i)}$.

6. Add some noise: Pick $0 \leq d \leq p^h - 2$ at random. Set $c_i = b_i + d$.

7. Public key - to be published: $c_0, c_1, \ldots, c_{p-1}; p, h$.

8. Private key - to be kept secret: t, g, π^{-1}, d.

Remark: Every user can use the *same* p and h. The probability of collisions (two users having the same keys) is negligible.

b. Encryption

To encrypt a binary message M of length p and weight (number of 1's) *exactly* h, add the c_i's whose corresponding bit is 1. Send

$$E(M) = c_{i_1} + c_{i_2} + \ldots + c_{i_h} \pmod{p^h - 1}.$$

c. Decryption

1. Let $r(t) = t^h \bmod f(t)$, a polynomial of degree $\leq h - 1$ (computed once at system generation).

2. Given $s = E(M)$, compute $s' = s - hd \pmod{p^h - 1}$.

3. Compute $q(t) = g^{s'} \bmod f(t)$, a polynomial of degree $h - 1$ in the formal variable t.

4. Add $t^h - r(t)$ to $q(t)$ to get $s(t) = t^h + q(t) - r(t)$, a polynomial of degree h in $GF(p)[t]$.

5. We now have
$$s(t) = (t + i_1) \cdot (t + i_2) \ldots (t + i_h)$$
namely $s(t)$ factors to *linear terms* over $GF(p)$. By successive substitutions, we find the h roots i_j's (at most p substitutions needed). Apply π^{-1} to recover the coordinates of the original M having the bit 1.

7.5 System Performance: Time, Space and Information Rate

In this section we analyze three basic parameters of the cryptosystem: The time needed for encrypting and decrypting a message, the size of the keys, and the information rate in terms of cleartext bits per ciphertext bits. The complexity of key generation is discussed in section 7.

Given a binary message length p and weight h, encrypting it amounts to adding h integers c_i, each smaller than p^h. The run time for decryption is much longer. It is dominated by the modular exponentiation: To raise a polynomial g to a power in the range $[1, p^h - 1]$ takes at most $2h \log p$ modular multiplications. The modulus is $f(t)$, a polynomial of degree h, with coefficients in $GF(p)$. Using the naive polynomial multiplication algorithm, $2h^2$ operations (in $GF(p)$) per modular multiplication will suffice. So overall, $4h^3 \log p$ operations in $GF(p)$ are required. For the proposed parameters $p \approx 200$, $h \approx 25$ this gives about 500,000 $GF(p)$ operations, and compares favorably with RSA encryption-decryption time.

The size of the keys, and especially of the public key, is an important factor in the design of any public key system. In our system, the size of the public key is that of p numbers, each in the range $[1, p^h - 1]$. In terms of bits, this is $p \log_2 p^h = ph \log_2 p$ bits. For $p \approx 200$, $h \approx 25$, the key takes less than 40,000 bits. While this number is about 35 times larger than the currently proposed size for the RSA public key (600 bits for the modulus and 600 for the exponent), it is still within practical bounds.

The information rate R of a block code is defined as $R = \frac{\log_2 |M|}{N}$, where $|M|$ is the size of the message space, and N is the number of bits in a ciphertext. Letting M range over all binary vectors of length p and weight h, $|M| = \binom{p}{h}$. $N = \log_2 p^h$, so the information rate is

$$R = \frac{\log \binom{p}{h}}{\log p^h}.$$

For the proposed parameters $p = 197$, $h = 24$, $R = 0.556$ (data expansion 1.798).

7.6 Transforming Unconstrained Bit Strings

We have assumed until now that the message space M contains binary vectors of length p and weight h. However, regular binary text does not have this form. This section contains a simple procedure for translating unconstrained binary text into the above form.

Given a binary text, we first break it into blocks of $\lfloor \log_2 \binom{p}{h} \rfloor$ bits each. Each such block is viewed as the binary representation of a number n, $0 \leq n < \binom{p}{h}$. To map these numbers into weight h binary vectors, we use the order preserving mapping induced by the lexicographic order of the vectors and the natural order of the integers. If n is larger than $\binom{p-1}{h-1}$, the first bit in the corresponding vector is set to 1. Otherwise, the first bit is set to 0. We then update p and h, and iterate p times, until all p bits are determined.

Code for transforming a number n into a binary vector $\vec{y}$

Input: n, p, h; Output: $\vec{y}$
1. **for** $i \leftarrow 1$ **to** p **do**
2.   **if** $n \geq \binom{p-i}{h}$ **then**
3. $y_i \leftarrow 1$
4. $n \leftarrow n - \binom{p-i}{h-1}$
5. $h \leftarrow h - 1$
6.   **else** $y_i \leftarrow 0$
7. **return** $\vec{y}$

The inverse transformation, which is the last step in decryption, is just as simple:

Code for transforming a binary vector $\vec{y}$ into a number n

Input: $\vec{y}, p, h$; Output: n
1. $n \leftarrow 0$
2. **for** $i \leftarrow 1$ **to** p **do**
3.   **if** $y_i = 1$ **then**
4. $n \leftarrow n + \binom{p-i}{h}$
5. $h \leftarrow h - 1$
6. **return** n

For efficient implementation, the $\frac{p \cdot h}{4}$ binomial coefficients preceding $\binom{p}{h}$ (in the Pascal triangle) will be precomputed and permanently stored.

Remark: The above indexing scheme is well known in the literature (see, e.g. [19]).

7.7 Proposed Parameters

As mentioned before, the main difficulty in implementing our cryptosystem is the computation of discrete logarithms in large finite fields $GF(p^h)$. This computational problem is considered quite hard in general. However, for some special cases, the algorithms of Coppersmith [18] and Pohlig and Hellman [38] work well in practice. Coppersmith's algorithm is appropriate for fields of small characteristic, and performs best in characteristic 2. Letting $p^h = 2^n$, the run time of the algorithm is $e^{O(\sqrt[3]{n \log^2 n})}$. For $n \leq 200$, implementation of the Coppersmith algorithm will terminate in a few hours on a mainframe computer. The Pohlig–Hellman algorithm works for any characteristic, provided $p^h - 1$ has only small prime factors. It turns out that the Pohlig–Hellman algorithm is preferable for our specific application, due to two properties: The nice factorization of several numbers $p^h - 1$ of appropriate magnitude, and the simplicity of the algorithm.

The Pohlig–Hellman algorithm has a $T \cdot S$ (time·space) complexity proportional to the largest factor of $p^h - 1$. While in general numbers whose order of magnitude is $\approx 200^{25}$ do not have 'small' largest factors (the expected size of the largest factor of a random number m is about $m^{0.6}$ – see Knuth and Pardo [30]), things are much better when the number has the form $x^h - 1$, since we can first factor this expression as a polynomial in x, and then factor each term as a number after substituting $x \leftarrow p$. Numbers h's with "good" factorization are especially effective. For example, $x^{24} - 1$ has the factors $x^8 - x^4 + 1$, $x^4 - x^2 + 1$, $x^4 + 1$, and other terms of degree not exceeding 2. Substituting $p = 197$, the largest prime factor of $197^{24} - 1$ is $10,316,017 \approx 10^7$. The square root of this is $3 \cdot 10^3$, so the Pohlig–Hellman algorithm can easily be implemented on a minicomputer within a few CPU hours for all the 197 logarithms.

Other possible values are (the last two values are from [13]):

- $p = 211$, $h = 24$ (largest prime factor of $211^{24} - 1$ is $216,330,241 \approx 2 \cdot 10^8$)
- $p = 243 = 3^5$, $h = 24$ (largest prime factor of $3^{120} - 1$ is $47,763,361 \approx 5 \cdot 10^7$).
- $p = 256 = 2^8$, $h = 25$ (largest prime factor of $2^{200} - 1$ is $3,173,389,601 \approx 3 \cdot 10^9$). This candidate has the advantage that the field is of characteristic 2. Thus binary arithmetic can be used for key generation and decryption

calculations. In addition, binary arithmetic offers easier implementation in special-purpose hardware.

7.8 Implementation Details

The key generation step was implemented on a Symbolics 3600 Lisp Machine. Polynomials were represented as arrays, and some preprocessing was done to speed-up the field arithmetic. In the implementation of the Pohlig–Hellman algorithm, instead of sorting the pre-computed powers, they were hashed in a 197-by-197 array according to the free term and the coefficient of t in the polynomial. This way the matching trials were simplified. However, one simple computation was not done in the preprocessing stage – computing successive squares of the generator $g, g^2, g^{2^2}, g^{2^3}, \ldots, g^{2^{182}}$ ($182 = \lfloor \log_2 197^{24} \rfloor$).

The overall run time for finding all 197 logarithms in $GF(197^{24})$ was about 8 hours. With some simple modifications, we expect that the above time can be reduced by 30 percent. It seems that even for $GF(256^{25})$ the computation should be feasible, taking advantage of the binary operations in the polynomial arithmetic. All these estimates can be drastically reduced if the computation is to be carried out on a faster, larger computer using a programming language more suitable for numerical calculations (e.g. Fortran).

CHAPTER 8

POSSIBLE ATTACKS

In this chapter we examine some possible attacks on the cryptosystem. We start with specialized attacks on the cryptosystem, where the cryptanalyst is trying to reconstruct the secret key (possibly with some partial knowledge of it). We proceed by considering low density and brute force attacks with no prior secret information, where the goal is not to reconstruct the secret key but rather to decipher a given ciphertext.

8.1 Specialized Attacks

a. Known g and d.

Given d, compute $\{b_0, b_1, \ldots, b_{p-1}\} = \{c_0 - d, c_1 - d, \ldots, c_{p-1} - d\}$. Let $t' = g^{b_0}$. Since $g^{a_0} - g^{b_0} = t - t' \in GF(p)$, the sets $\{t+i | i \in GF(p)\}$ and $\{t'+i | i \in GF(p)\}$ are identical. Thus, for every $i \in GF(p)$ there is a unique $\sigma(i) \in GF(p)$ so that $g^{b_{\sigma(i)}} = t' + i$. Using t', g, σ and d, the cryptanalyst can perform the same decryption algorithm as the legitimate reciever.

b. Known t and d.

Pick arbitrary generator g'. Compute $a'_i = \log_{g'}(t+i)$. As sets, we have

$$\{c_0 - d, c_1 - d, \ldots, c_{p-1} - d\} = \{a_0, a_1, \ldots, a_{p-1}\}$$
$$= L\{a'_0, a'_1, \ldots, a'_{p-1}\}$$

where equality is modulo $p^h - 1$, the numbers $L, p^h - 1$ are relatively prime, and L satisfies $g = g'^L$. Once L is recovered, we are done, for then $g = g'^L$, and we can reconstruct π and have all the pieces of the private key.

If one of the a'_i (a'_0, say) is relatively prime to $p^h - 1$, then L is one of $a_j a'_0{}^{-1}$ (mod $p^h - 1$) for some $0 \leq j \leq p - 1$. Otherwise, the cryptanalyst can compute

L modulo each of the prime power factors of $p^h - 1$ (which, by the choice of p and h, are all small and therefore easy to find), and then combine them together using the Chinese remainder theorem.

c. Known t (attack due to Oded Goldreich).

Pick arbitrary generator g'. Compute $a'_i = \log_{g'}(t+i)$. As sets, we have

$$\{c_0 - c_0, c_1 - c_0, \ldots, c_{p-1} - c_0\} = \{a_0 - a_0, a_1 - a_0, \ldots, a_{p-1} - a_0\}$$
$$= L\{a'_0 - a'_0, a'_1 - a'_0, \ldots, a'_{p-1} - a'_0\}$$

and now it is possible to proceed as in (b).

d. Known permutation π and d (attack due to Andrew Odlyzko).

Since the knapsack is dense, there are small integral coefficients x_i (some of which may be negative) such that

$$\sum_{i=0}^{p-1} x_i a_i = 0$$

(see appendix 2 and (e) for a justification to this claim). The x_i's can be efficiently found by applying the Lenstra-Lenstra-Lovasz basis reduction algorithm [32] to a the truncated Lagarias-Odlyzko lattice (see appendix 2, and [37] for a similar attack on other knapsack schemes). Raising g to both sides of the last equality, we get

$$g^{\sum_{i=0}^{p-1} x_i a_i} = 1$$

i.e.

$$\prod_{i=0}^{p-1} (t+i)^{x_i} = 1 \ .$$

The left hand side of the last equality is a rational function of t. The generator g, which is still unknown, is not a part of the equality. If $m_1 = |\sum x_i^+|$ ($m_2 = |\sum x_i^-|$) denotes the sum of positive (negative) x_i's, and $m = \max(m_1, m_2)$, then we get a polynomial equation of degree $m - 1$ in t, with coefficients from $GF(p)$. Since the x_i's are small, m is also not too large. All roots (in $GF(p^h)$) of this polynomial can be found using a fast probabilistic algorithm. The element t is necessarily one of these roots, so attack (c) can now be used.

The most efficient way for root finding which we know of (Rabin [40]) requires finding the gcd of $g(t)$ and t^{p^h-1}, where $g(t) = \prod_{i=0}^{p-1}(t+i)^{x_i} - 1$. With $p^h - 1 \gg m$, this polynomial gcd computation is performed by raising t to the power $p^h - 1$ and reducing modulo $g(t)$. So we basically have to perform $h \log_2 p$ multiplications of m degree polynomials with coefficients in $GF(p)$, and reducing modulo $g(t)$ each time. Assuming standard arithmetic, each polynomial multiplication will take m^2 $GF(p)$ operations (FFT arithmetic [see, e.g. 1, ch. 7] will introduce a large constant and will probably be less efficient in practice). Thus the root finding algorithm will require at least $m^2 h \log_2 p$ operations in $GF(p)$ (assuming that a single root is found).

Remark: If π is not known, this attack does not seem to work since, even though the x_i can be found, they give rise to an 'unknown' polynomial. If $m_1 + m_2$ is very small then one can try all $\binom{p}{m_1+m_2}$ possibilities even without knowing π. However, with π unknown and $m_1 + m_2$ exceeding 10, this brute force approach becomes infeasible. A more refined method for dealing with unknown π is presented next.

e. Nothing Known (attack due to Ernest Brickell).

This attack is a continuation to Odlyzko's attack. The goal is again to find a small degree equation satisfied by g. Using a carefully designed lattice, it is possible to find integer coefficients x_i, many of them 0, such that both equations

$$\sum_{i=0}^{p-1} x_i c_i \equiv 0 \pmod{p^h - 1}$$

$$\sum_{i=0}^{p-1} x_i \equiv 0 \pmod{p^h - 1}$$

hold. The second equality guarantees that

$$g^{\sum_{i=0}^{p-1} x_i c_i} = g^{\sum_{i=0}^{p-1} x_i (b_i + d)}$$
$$= g^{\sum_{i=0}^{p-1} x_i b_i} \cdot g^{d \sum_{i=0}^{p-1} x_i}$$
$$= g^{\sum_{i=0}^{p-1} x_i b_i}$$

and thus, by the first equality,

$$g^{\sum_{i=0}^{p-1} x_i b_i} = 1 ,$$

that is $g^{\sum_{i=0}^{p-1} x_i a_{\pi(i)}} = 1$.

With the permutation π unknown, this equality now means

$$\prod_{i=0}^{p-1} (t + \pi(i))^{x_i} = 1 .$$

Let $g_\pi(t) = \prod_{i=0}^{p-1} (t + \pi(i))^{x_i} - 1$, and ℓ be the number of non-zero x_i's. Every one-to-one mapping from the set $\{i \mid x_i \neq 0\}$ into $\{0, 1, \ldots, p-1\}$ gives rise to a different polynomial in $g_\pi(t)$. Only the "correct" polynomial will have the right t as one of its roots. Thus on the average we have to try $\frac{1}{2} \frac{p!}{(p-\ell)!}$ mappings to come up with the right polynomial. (In fact it suffices to consider the mappings of only $\ell - 1$ elements, since having $t + j$ for some $j \in GF(p)$ is as good as having t itself, and so $\frac{1}{2} \frac{p!}{(p-\ell+1)!}$ mappings are to be checked).

For every such mapping, the cryptanalyst should find the roots in $GF(p^h)$ of $g_\pi(t)$, an m degree polynomial with coefficients from $GF(p)$ (m denotes here the same quantity as in (d)). Combining the calculations above with the running-time estimates for polynomial arithmetic, the expected running-time for recovering t will thus be $\frac{1}{2} \frac{p!}{(p-\ell+1)!} \cdot m^2 h \log_2 p$ ($GF(p)$ operations). There is a trade-off between ℓ and m. Consider the ℓ non-zero x_i's. How large do they have to be in order to have a non-zero solution to $\sum x_i a_i \equiv 0 \pmod{p^h - 1}$? If the x_i's are bound in the range $\frac{-B}{2} < x_i < \frac{B}{2}$ then this gives us B^ℓ combinations of $\sum x_i a_i$. If $B^\ell > p^h - 1$, then two of these combinations *must* be the same modulo $p^h - 1$. In fact, if $B^\ell > p^{h/2}$ then by the birthday paradox two of the B^ℓ sums are going to be equal modulo $p^h - 1$ with probability no less than $\frac{1}{2}$. Assuming the later bound, $B \approx p^{h/2\ell}$. To get a non zero combination $\sum x_i a_i \equiv 0 \pmod{p^h - 1}$, we subtract two combinations with the same sum. The average absolute value of the resulting x_i is about $B/2 = \frac{p^{h/2\ell}}{2}$, and about half ($\ell/2$) of them are negative. Thus the the sum of negative (positive) x_i's is $m \sim \frac{\ell p^{h/2\ell}}{4}$. The total runnning-time for finding t is thus

$$\frac{1}{2}\frac{p!}{(p-\ell+1)!} \cdot m^2 h \log_2 p \sim \frac{1}{2}\frac{p!}{(p-\ell+1)!} \cdot \left(\frac{\ell p^{h/2\ell}}{4}\right)^2 h \log_2 p$$

$$\sim \frac{p^{\ell-1} p^{h/\ell} \ell^2 h \log_2 p}{32}$$

The above expression is optimized with $\ell = \theta(\sqrt{h})$, resulting in $O(p^{2\sqrt{h}} h^2 \log_2 p)$ algorithm for retrieving t. While this expression is asymptotically superior to all other methods mentioned above, it seems quite prohibitive in practice. For example, taking $p = 197$ and $h = 24$, $\ell - 1 + h/\ell$ is optimized at $\ell = 5$, yielding 8.8. But $197^{8.8} > 2^{60}$, so the attack is impractical. (Even assuming FFT arithmetic and complexity $O(m)$ for the root finding algorithm, the resulting expression $p^{\ell-1+h/2\ell} \ell h \log_2 p$ is optimized at $\ell = 3$ yielding about 2^{52}. The extra log factors of the FFT and the hidden constant will drive the expression up to at least 2^{58})

8.2 Low Density Attacks

In appendix 2 we give a description of the Lagarias–Odlyzko low density attack. The *density* $d(A)$ of a knapsack system $A = \{a_i | \ 0 \leq i \leq p-1\}$, is defined to be

$$d(A) = \frac{p}{\log_2(\max a_i)} \ .$$

Given a knapsack system $A = \{a_i | \ 0 \leq i \leq p-1\}$ and a sum instance (ciphertext) $S = \sum_{i=0}^{p-1} x_i a_i$, they construct a $p+1$ dimensional lattice. The lattice construction uses the p knapsack elements and the given ciphertext. A certain vector in this lattice (which we call here the *special vector*) is defined. This vector corresponds to the solution of the given ciphertext (yields the coefficients x_i in the sum), and the goal of the cryptanalyst is to find it. Lagarias and Odlyzko have shown that if $d(A)$ is low, this special vector is the shortest one in their lattice.

Using the last observation, what Lagarias and Odlyzko are trying to do is to find the shortest vector in the lattice. The tool they use is the basis reduction algorithm of Lenstra, Lenstra and Lovasz. While this algorithm usually succeeds if the shortest vector in the lattice is much shorter than all other vectors, it does not do so well if the shortest vector is relatively close in length to other vectors.

In our specific case, the knapsack has high density. The length (square of Euclidean norm) of the special vector will not be much shorter than the length of many other vectors (24 vs. 40 for $p = 197$, $h = 24$ – see appendix 2). Therefore the LLL algorithm, applied to the Lagarias–Odlyzko lattice, cannot be expected to find the special vector. Experiments, done by Andrew Odlyzko, on a smaller knapsack created by us support this claim. For the test case we've generated an instance of the knapsack with parameters $p = 103$ and $h = 12$. For these parameters the density is 1.271. Using the calculations of [31], the length of the shortest non-special vector in the constructed lattice should be at least 17. However, the LLL algorithm did not find the special vector even when its length was only 5 (i.e. when only 5 knapsack elements were added together in the sum). So, it seems that for the Lagarias–Odlyzko attack to be successful against our system, it must use a better shortest vector algorithm. Currently, the best (exact) shortest vector algorithm known is the one of Kannan [28], and its performance is no better, in our application, than the brute force attack sketched in section 4.

In the following section we point out that it is possible to make the special vector which solves a given ciphertext longer than the shortest vector in the Lagarias–Odlyzko lattice. However, with the current state of shortest vector algorithms, it looks like such modification to the cryptosystem is not really needed.

8.3 Countermeasures Against Shortest Vector Attacks

Let $\vec{x}$ be the special vector which yields the decryption of a specific ciphertext. In the previous section we argued that with the proposed parameters, the special vector $\vec{x}$ will not be much shorter than many other lattice vectors. In this section we suggest a slight change in the encryption procedure. This change will have the effect of making $\vec{x}$ *longer* than many other lattice vectors. The change will also reduce the information rate of the system, but its density will not be changed.

To demonstrate this idea, let us first ignore the restrictions in the choice of h and p. Suppose we handle n-dimensional knapsacks with $h = n/\log_2 n$. By taking $n/(2\log_2 n)$ elements with multiplicity 1, and $\frac{n}{2\log_2^2 n}$ with multiplicity $\log_2 n$, $\vec{x}$ will have length

$$\frac{n}{2\log_2 n} + \frac{n\log_2^2 n}{2\log_2^2 n} = \frac{n}{2\log_2 n} + \frac{n}{2}$$

The density of such knapsack will be

$$\frac{n}{\log_2 n^{n/\log_2 n}} = 1$$

By the heuristic argument of Lagarias and Odlyzko [31], n-dimensional lattices with density 1 will contain many vectors of length shorter than $n/4$. Since the length of the special vector $\vec{x}$ is more than twice $n/4$, the Lagarias–Odlyzko method will not find $\vec{x}$.

The idea of increasing the length of the special vector by using several knapsack items with repetitions is applicable for the proposed parameters of the actual system. For $n = 197$, $h = 24$, the following encryption method can be used: Take 8 knapsack elements with multiplicity 1, and 8 knapsack elements with multiplicity 2. The length of the special vector $\vec{x}$ is then $1 \cdot 8 + 2^2 \cdot 8 = 40$. We substitute these arguments in the formulae of [31]. The critical density is 1.073 (see appendix 2). This means that (for large enough n), n-dimensional Lagarias–Odlyzko lattices with density exceeding 1.073 are expected to have many vectors of length $< 40n/197$. The density of our lattice is

$$\frac{197}{\log_2 197^{24}} = \frac{197}{24 \cdot \log_2 197} = 1.077$$

and so is strictly greater than the critical density. We expect the lattice to contain many vectors of length < 40 (provided 197 is "large enough" and our lattice behaves "normally"). Thus the Lagarias–Odlyzko attack is not expected to find $\vec{x}$ even with an exact shortest vector algorithm at its disposal.

Of course, countermeasures can also be countered. Other lattices which are tailored to our scheme (rather than the general Lagarias–Odlyzko lattice) can be constructed and have better performance. For example, Don Coppersmith suggested to modify the Lagarias-Odlyzko lattice so that short vectors also satisfy $\sum x_i = h$ (see appendix 2). For the parameters $p = 197, h = 24$, it is more likely that the shortest vector in the modified lattice will be the special vector which solves the ciphertext. In addition, for these specific parameters, our modified encryption might cause brute-force algorithms to have better chance of success. It is possible that by working in larger fields (e.g. $GF(256^{25})$) we may remedy these problems, but we did not pursue this issue any further.

8.4 Brute Force Attacks

Despite the sophistication of the previous attacks, none of them outperforms a careful brute-force attack (unless the cryptanalyst is supplied with some part of the secret decryption key). The most efficient method we know of for solving knapsack instances with h out of p items, given a specific ciphertext, is the following: There are $\binom{p}{h}$ ways of choosing h out of p elements. Take a random subset S containing $p/2$ elements. The probability that a given sum contains exactly $h/2$ out of these $p/2$ elements is

$$\frac{\binom{p/2}{h/2}^2}{\binom{p}{h}} \approx \frac{1}{\sqrt{h}}.$$

Assuming that this is indeed the case, we generate all $h/2$ sums of S and of its complement, and sort them. The goal is to find a pair of sums from the two lists whose sum matches the desired target. This can be achieved by keeping two pointers to the two lists, and marching linearly through each (one in increasing order, and the other in decreasing order). If the two lists are exhausted but no matching sum was found, then another random S is tried. The run time per one choice of S is dominated by sorting all $h/2$ sums of both S and its complement.

This will require $2 \cdot \binom{p/2}{h/2} \ln \binom{p/2}{h/2}$ operations. On the average, about $\sqrt{h}$ choices of S have to be made. The overall expected running time will thus be

$$2 \cdot \binom{p/2}{h/2} \ln \binom{p/2}{h/2} \frac{\binom{p}{h}}{\binom{p/2}{h/2}^2} = \frac{2 \binom{p}{h} \ln \binom{p/2}{h/2}}{\binom{p/2}{h/2}} .$$

For the proposed parameters $p = 197, h = 24$, the expected number of operations is $3.466 \cdot 10^{17} > 2^{58}$, so such brute force attack is impractical. The knapsack algorithm of Schroeppel and Shamir [44] might be used here for space efficiency. However, its run time behavior is no better than the above algorithm.

8.5 A Word of Caution

Even though none of these attacks seems to produce a serious threat to the system security, other attacks might be successful. We urge the reader to examine our proposal for as yet undiscovered weaknesses.

APPENDIX 1

On Discrete Logarithms and Factorization

We'll show here how the problem of factoring "paired primes modulus" $N = p \cdot q$ (where p, q primes) is polynomially reducible to that of finding indices ("logarithms") in Z_N. Let $a \in Z_N^*$ be chosen at random. Since $a^{\varphi(N)} = 1 \pmod{N}$, we have

$$a^N = a^{N-\varphi(N)} = a^{pq-(p-1)(q-1)} = a^{p+q-1} \pmod{N}.$$

The index of a^{p+q-1} to base a is defined as the minimal exponent e which satisfies $a^e = a^{p+q-1} \pmod{N}$. With reasonable probability, e equals $p+q-1$. In such case, a discrete logarithm subroutine will output $p+q-1$ when given $a^N \mod N$ as input. Having $N = p \cdot q$ and $p+q-1$, p and q can easily be determined.

The "reasonable probability" is bounded below by the probability that $a \mod p$ is a multiplicative generator of Z_p^*, and $a \mod q$ is a multiplicative generator of Z_q^*. These two events are independent, and each of them individually has reasonable probability to happen. Thus both happen with "reasonable probability". Let c denote the gcd of $p-1$ and $q-1$. Assume, without loss of generality, that $q < p$. Furthermore, assume that $c < q-1$ (this is "usually" the case, and in particular holds for RSA moduli, where both $p-1$ and $q-1$ have large random prime factors). The congruence $a^e = a^{p+q-1} \pmod{N}$ implies $a^e = a^{p+q-1} \pmod{p}$ and $a^e = a^{p+q-1} \pmod{q}$, so from the fact that a is a generator modulo both p and q, we get

$$e \equiv p+q-1 \pmod{p-1}$$
$$e \equiv p+q-1 \pmod{q-1}$$

and thus $e - (p+q-1) \equiv 0 \pmod{(p-1)(q-1)/c}$ $\quad (*)$.

Since $c = \gcd(p-1, q-1) \leq (q-1)/2$, we have $(p-1)(q-1)/c \geq 2(p-1) > p+q-1$. Combining the last inequality with $(*)$, we get $e - (p+q-1) = 0$, or $e = p+q-1$, as desired.

APPENDIX 2

THE LAGARIAS–ODLYZKO LOW DENSITY ATTACK

In this appendix we give a brief description of the Lagarias–Odlyzko "low-density" attack, which is based on finding short vectors in lattices. (A different "low density" attack was proposed by Brickell [11].) Given a knapsack system $A = \{a_i | \ 0 \leq i \leq n - 1\}$ and a sum instance $S = \sum_{i=0}^{n-1} x_i a_i$, the algorithm proceeds as follows:

a) Construct an $n + 1$ dimensional integer lattice with basis vectors

$$\vec{v}_0 = (1, 0, 0, \ldots, 0, a_0)$$
$$\vec{v}_1 = (0, 1, 0, \ldots, 0, a_1)$$
$$\vec{v}_2 = (0, 0, 1, \ldots, 0, a_2)$$
$$\vdots$$
$$\vec{v}_{n-1} = (0, 0, 0, \ldots, 1, a_{n-1})$$
$$\vec{v}_n = (0, 0, 0, \ldots, 0, -S)$$

b) Look for the shortest non-zero vector $\vec{u}$ in this lattice. This step is using the LLL basis reduction algorithm which finds a relatively short vector in the lattice (even though no proof that the shortest vector will be produced by the LLL algorithm is known, and in fact this need not be the case).

c) Check if $\vec{u} = \vec{x}$, where $\vec{x} = (x_0, x_1, x_2, \ldots, x_{n-1}, 0)$ is the special vector which deciphers S.

We'll call the lattice spanned by the $n + 1$ basis vectors the *full Lagarias–Odlyzko lattice*, and the sublattice spanned by the first n basis vectors the *truncated* Lagarias–Odlyzko lattice. The truncated lattice does not depend on the actual sum S. The basic idea behind the algorithm is that since $S = \sum x_i a_i$,

$\vec{x}$ is always a vector in the space spanned by the basis vectors. The Euclidean norm of $\vec{x}$ is $\sqrt{\sum_{i=0}^{n-1} x_i^2}$. Lagarias and Odlyzko show that for almost all sets A (in an appropriate probability space) whose density is less than 0.645, there will be a unique vector in the lattice spanned by $\vec{v}_0, \vec{v}_1, \ldots .\vec{v}_n$ with Euclidean norm not exceeding $\sqrt{n/2}$.

More precisely, let

$$\theta(z) = 1 + 2 \sum_{i=1}^{\infty} z^{i^2}$$

$$\delta(\alpha, x) = \alpha x + \log_e \theta\left(e^{-x}\right)$$

$$\delta(\alpha, x_\alpha) = \min_{x \geq 0} \delta(\alpha, x)$$

$$d_\alpha^{-1} = (\log_2 e) \cdot \delta(\alpha, x_\alpha)$$

Then for $n \to \infty$, for almost all n-dimensional knapsacks of density $d(A) < d_\alpha$, all the non-zero vectors in the truncated lattice have length $> \alpha \cdot n$. Thus if the special vector $\vec{x}$ is of length $< \alpha \cdot n$, it will be the shortest vector in the full lattice. Plugging in $\alpha = 1/2$, one gets $x_{1/2} = 0.9979$ and $\log_2 e \cdot \delta(1/2, x_{1/2}) = 1.547$. So $d_{1/2} = 1.547^{-1} = 0.645$. Similarly, $d_{1/4} = 0.94$. Thus if $||\vec{x}||^2 \leq n/2$ and $d(A) \leq 0.645$, a shortest vector algorithm will find $\vec{x}$ (similarly if $||\vec{x}||^2 \leq n/4$ and $d(A) \leq 0.94$). Lagarias and Odlyzko conjectured that the above densities are "cut-off" densities in the following sense: Almost all knapsacks A with $d(A) > d_\alpha$ will have exponentially many vectors with Euclidean norm $\leq \sqrt{\alpha \cdot n}$ in the truncated lattice. These short vectors correspond to small linear dependencies among the a_i's – solutions to $\sum_{i=0}^{p-1} x_i a_i = 0$ with small integral x_i's (not necessarily ± 1 or 0).

For 0 – 1 knapsack problems, the Euclidean norm of $\vec{x}$ is not too big since each coordinate contributes at most 1 to the sum. However, if the same item is taken more than once, the norm of $\vec{x}$ grows substantially. This is the basis for the modification in section 8.3. For the parameter $\alpha = 40/197$ (corresponding to a special vector of length 40 in a 197-dimensional lattice), we compute

$$\min_{x \geq 0} \delta(\alpha, x) = \delta(\alpha, 2.070)$$
$$= 0.646$$

so the critical density is

$$d_\alpha = (\log_2 e \cdot 0.646)^{-1}$$
$$= 1.073 \ .$$

To make use of the additional information that in our ciphertexts $\sum_{i=0}^{p-1} x_i = h$, Coppersmith suggested to add one more column to the basis elements in the Lagarias–Odlyzko lattice. For $i = 0, 1 \ldots n-1$, $\vec{v}_i$ will have a large constant s in this additional entry, while $\vec{v}_n$ will contain $-hs$ in this entry ($s \approx 10$ suffices for our application). To be shorter than the special vector, a vector $\vec{y}$ in the truncated lattice must now satisfy both $\sum_{i=0}^{p-1} y_i = 0$ and $\sum_{i=0}^{p-1} y_i a_i = 0$.

APPENDIX 3

A Specific Public Key

This appendix contain an example of the public key computed in $GF(197^{24})$. The knapsack elements are listed below. This is a full version of the cryptosystem, with the elements permuted and $d \neq 0$. It is proposed as a test case for cryptanalytic attacks against our system. A file which contains these numbers can be electronically transferred by request from the author of this thesis.

```
165918055388861881050470305450301538114795999009168334 5
890460357374644239212231641853962216769858475492050049 1
686942289098203883065173332109406486047654504905051023 6
884350181670319947847463860625624937447231583872321268 7
273085211853095557657927451499434236517420912511363175
191713483800032854166688672011640804882705898909748271 8
371048240292386832980224946455594928214392771549277566 8
298720766472653117124532003628229729534286526730739857 7
388776666444946756737255446394801075902848761246743865 5
532957598947500840506641574190261215023927685844775 58
945043542698087649915054552646048460374160692269665087 6
450557525840744842996537290250219903294557697178457172
287994755035332983092976037422343775448034197189536263
101184017646464822525333786200873926303826639882586624 25
549453385137036580581816180532850555838963733836284273 3
660051136374072429718266066786207813907122130719679721 7
459378260963144816109734442229407083191352920821647999
170529313321117767925100118685360647431629637266557746 3
529693225768383586845576970364037383991622366077672422 6
466064163429815363796924737370550476569334637366644 21
531717028702161197761257959383599550989596093806687469 4
954700703625702197881077479244434886304508346703042216 4
873991872977731880522007469795844297344486466731386716 7
121893545970680060882400763245092942338481701421418703 6
643579292244760045876785403402932897033404749504174150 4
408203310163483080692114127373748300577887699738237957 0
```

A KNAPSACK-TYPE CRYPTOSYSTEM

3476840117822498384453797608352249452261755574946436
10775143624182084460146514690774520411115991214477052529
7363672187196151096263068583933635874162043800628565542
6132911186848723392017074802347613026512261764800254957
4621452836237129572668766922737559587573084329705006138
3080212245061335648175456777189565846347127068099687309
1006924652892244379525577705820891605807301698209566063
1239188873372458722449930677483901206097805669939533233
8290927400902143008887128916044001178904661328310569128
5714432420745902617149738940321959487572283803340465152
4338432111441836091889594082303270707084733947396101241
5321610236079748192040737134454717995542276347795910409
4937367917163847304913811853806699997767089532519223065
6610823000041678448002462502266524169680630816638103863
7262818004742619896833158988336732204289317194153575691
2502947348371780914313064990139029216175066263151770147
1117308630302592623903026436611637003318498250581945681
3478556997627898249717209595998962919368456813037741 38
3984202202810239637041527156629398387293462547124656184
9568120289176334697968798749514649180114650583753072227
1301300995092594924016761451746735550321678103621738066
5699235330321470828600612638889384069110659050284600816
8878620549807995478768677230741624150433622110531693925
3463049994770925147816582669932423724431599459976702144
1634420533780126860220986928711573687757577853822370501
4131920160915650780822086028657914715776446242012691750
1362047942896581988244999836237461442735494739210489808
9430250728075275781274743286984722213290652553684465820
6280141388001593623959448900856171987015212445806250560
1149112544402224179082211201257337711885676220572223370
3519675004644133101803802941360148055171987581452853803
7820667368140962900282720639234452600820532123646041563
1096643581992920614132756640235483804563423386155494340
9941933529523876933598787307173548868167610719273363866
3876101494866729880497511938408978211301061936560811675
88926096991208511339179170818227049595008637330329677229
7092060679521818036621321555550639594833422393607231579
4400804658324132179154935594022157397198137892043978814
2003567532995305455043180101111935807943047847306518004
1072572555735644837484001489488939256966261516503325641
4718681518838132526024557001023842008895466881040494467
9782714587940929563127945903276594874240059681011363698
7221487726451204266080463876115882926947703571776633959
8340628407032059861351234625548370525044335145545866216

```
10697186315110563324293407333965300526490994463025514775
76483167130504063640319974031851613156263454423877073
48773713131185257187230019419241831040101561144032109 43
55891673162835686061291552175617004798713104731148 61372
57604021900794789772902419039482095667963005840365 60255
16344118087140807261845807642056674279028396687558 64462
59079108698010912614126453231520270285202883652820 22791
10331038587940102685121128504609262772340293128223506833
57264154824339565943594123898369497786320418753484 23101
10397842526836530713589437056977511941286325611927173291
88956910404259369927773424716715295482002594565110 18046
11476697198084608347001085696021116568979308201540 223885
45176885062053273325238708224128072407897952981849221
33520122457007346720812607233107607378225167805232 98120
84480953798142617218659133189706126805247227756367 10182
93048465007553709302427950040771156237848424812079 34659
35835850555708627150506308931794853232411048702618 3317
88380414179645500467180984461502469487419879959715 62145
61362558648700404907279151410276904306163560648456 44806
69068549964187988903491610393619104850189460669943 52581
10170413544474167073889406955767321697221405994911 185878
96405151196412540174267172670860225223363900723653 17157
30381094573979368369848170112708378474904842678392 1481
65953944526860455162708997912325021866871432371953 04272
15898415667085714169417570895421266540065201467974 25083
11085664727759733005620644294861047610034453223469 425035
75350596770313992090054754153804015826383809005567 70350
82001421541581813556096247735599601882754484766066 84965
20097126900624341026856759550223327025601457079702 24453
10568688041667857314452197491559730299422286309282 738674
10611062465304524980299936816158445724082435571522 23554
95212615335262052266281003127920841203262259104902 03709
85825303825022144924556017711409849710653605354922 64971
65013325812043463030795151537279049386803257885823 29269
33177142766791266491485489105489589474963766697391 11369
48741329115129286520666748141381958185978939834169 56618
85001228526982733607238552510805714279785812964433 00871
46558880238988643770134830681201665396494051882240 3803
38196860068272378748938575226075757047064249287481 35743
24455061815105433480919468601394208474961563114023 17416
49715670160910822324832667703288631975971722225510 33762
12626096488792705363382786376721783115036393783167 62898
10880314738320559788385102529426564253426264142547 211799
38886882032184393547173282307245877596336259407505 36816
```

10860128816246376835396650892423492833238996106962188108
937015345161745308557155376907542479090922419179647454
503282478660902598216077760177782599503793987267246479
7951682246278723195457177501681939589674822136739853974
5463500835616440109490581965761882164871292581416770541
2954540015836809838923994897090519106458324851302017933
9104861272595347035407604442082821339674724178236829843
4276004090546060553469690096659082633166104531677031316
8920549264928769763742925160432454320437900897897145620
11618630840955246608355771374831822847853081125184373290
3823867726368698856614979064702978458012600631274415877
8671737361545103697852647258515398947803516638145273291
499166921011730697434945051278016702024221484712594454
5915598711080735606129613661456327944406858964435154667
8173498654318327586943649747916018347200281212689047290
7275595429446182302879669944077095261926983310050621817
8200988174711899297550763593522027263904422925378960992
11259346252873044495915049754437393362171010088512550082
2002368795089233775442710203575437096591528513855693285
9273646744933903888135623428241819858280355170938205124
10928596465390575301307994873245167040059050147403733262
11507588820870116335321813443702739933780393408655812377
10785501785425425687964232314342101054761852867034564690
8937011647607496047515341562814494889237585386748941847
4394604991486329175708242631515782649023799357464726926
8409235957266821788960831580264731332474188602137707600
3728643452352018700840852096041193711402328567048040022
8272326742062489089809029789407534709776378835911312941
701377935237711726780832198631114938381571173881097663
4217271510299422316513539263935119232604857080751496559
8780957254540706500170750823867567401772539267267905370
170059311803762518939184815879698865087119140633996907
3864583323966915577606862257189742149210357433211871552
8473537958074036950094577844741929015845100045286152185
536459022346820368385578548808352992733402170168236436
11184499462288968070754455605229210932516750553409455798
1207951324289711166036697717046456099940468532934008002
1620207483168538885285524176342342715115767110103890963
9419113975870798390150760064851666450072819106900418278
5047061323668627906678255313661984091040986771426248661
4455715808568444126463792240767530160024239783146027287
2055708583094748127433520562049415256330509144335677370
822142663443212777645857532426265323721039040163355885
6327660152172723221702320871134172541113116074530751289

```
1161820407394597453217947475892232939576692293418388537 3
2681284829731657909799375030584463351722802694145504145
6049349233223855032140569250300226010438472844901345207
5653188878279392627297817877052771841176800457209818460
8746971498576924580862790073519261903224815996766650636
7707851868801266859527003522562026900874057533615974848
3379208175720838995972371245424813264780695540329883333
4191411226738609897786638402978981306173058319645577920
1021170816510485405720209559463776452548901374855036971 4
6980278166263928822410341894296642109825545586477476070
1847955825021785896447787560851214349928735795947671125
2734203200200558271382358178082463795634346967137177307
1087027301152196932637158545367923526203515457307186945 6
7220668587256604649775201135599337026837426113444289998
2805584377506127501253310897603956581444682504722824588
7617604224852838099708238920029691931830181900119468485
4852828442927974331206739154786746857916171958420537633
5597325117167958891635340527133426280020727951618666449
5058448763337068787757309487214319452724492848947048850
4836045376818476982118583337126970966350793318872412198
2838492198009993978308530616995674842114117845715972 2
7521830908610065824407290097000507716947796032485903 2
4627571935515247312390461614145879081244359702203606 45
3548316079628564518391086386772280206468827682110383051
2082005476582188454956618747601842210928057329483120854
1019783514928405665435564578591675390320445666808801512 6
4636092812212026895621740261870820526242448468160600010
3125818616334663903640293286981232105491162115909170351
1134421672856835118408958787881894427305182403607066582
1123871123105629776096812032755453064495838161676788187
5794050479015248291325502007300813968634856736211580022
4494655107601102037208333662312535245041777695947383166
9119204763142813562838438103855186160266236020445373601
2252273840245809422997790979417862651953946579056544432
7699136983782470018675579966330989232306312887731069424
5298532149479734331583109594640198858682133562901258825
8904753708068623153941993185049726417000501976266416274
1322575616024132593704279643926904588928166184734844702
4550372378328108483134988054103459460650586154311332 58
```

REFERENCES

[1] Aho, A., J. Hopcroft, and J. Ullman, *The design and analysis of computer algorithms*, Addison-Wesley, Reading, 1974.

[2] Alexi, W., B. Chor, O. Goldreich, and C. P. Schnorr, "RSA and Rabin functions: Certain parts are as hard as the whole", to appear in *SIAM Jour. on Computing*, extended abstract in *Proc. of the 25th IEEE Symp. on Foundation of Computer Science*, 1984, pp. 449-457.

[3] Ben-Or, M., B. Chor, and A. Shamir, "On the Cryptographic Security of Single RSA Bits", *15th ACM Symp. on Theory of Computation*, April 1983, pp. 421-430.

[4] Blum, M., "Coin flipping by telephone: A protocol for solving impossible problems", *IEEE Spring COMCON*, pp. 133–137, 1982.

[5] Blum, L., M. Blum, and M. Shub, "Comparison of Two Pseudo- Random Number Generators", *Advances in Cryptology: Proceedings of Crypto82*, Chaum,D., et al. eds., Plenum Press, 1983, pp. 61-79.

[6] Blum,M. and S. Goldwasser, "An Efficient Probabilistic PKCS as Secure as Factoring", *Advances in Cryptology: Proceedings of Crypto84*, G.R. Blakely and D. Chaum. eds., Springer–Verlag, 1985, pp. 288–299.

[7] Blum,M. and S. Micali, "How to Generate Cryptographically Strong Sequences of Pseudo-Random Bits", *SIAM Jour. on Computing*, vol. 13 no. 4, pp. 850–864, November 1984.

[8] Bose, R.C. and S. Chowla, "Theorems in the additive theory of numbers", *Comment. Math. Helvet.*, vol. 37, pp. 141–147, 1962.

[9] Brent, R.P. and H.T. Kung, "Systolic VLSI arrays for linear time gcd computation", *VLSI 83, IFIP*, F. Anceau and E.J. Aas (eds.), pp. 145–154, Elsevier Science Publishers B.V., 1983.

[10] Brickell, E.F., "A new knapsack based cryptosystem", Presented in Crypto83 rump session.

[11] Brickell, E.F., "Are most low density knapsacks solvable in polynomial time?", *Proceedings of the Fourteenth Southeastern Conference*

[12] Brickell, E.F., "Breaking iterated knapsacks", *Advances in Cryptology: Proceedings of Crypto84*, G.R. Blakely and D. Chaum. eds., Springer–Verlag, 1985, pp. 342–358.

[13] Brillhart, J., D.H. Lehmer, J.L. Selfridge, B. Tuckerman and S.S. Wagstaff, Jr., *Factorization of $b^n \pm 1$*, in *Contemporary Mathematics*, vol. 22, AMS, Providence, 1983.

[14] Chor, B. and O. Goldreich, "RSA/Rabin least significant bits are $\frac{1}{2} + \frac{1}{poly(n)}$ secure", *Advances in Cryptology: Proceedings of Crypto84*, G.R. Blakely and D. Chaum. eds., Springer–Verlag, 1985, pp. 303–313. (Also available as Technical memo TM-260, Laboratory for Computer Science, MIT, May 1984.)

[15] Chor, B., O. Goldreich, and S. Goldwasser, "The bit security of modular squaring given a partial factorization of the modulus", to appear in the proceedings of *Crypto85*.

[16] Chor, B., S. Goldwasser, S. Micali, and B. Awerbuch, "Verifiable secret sharing and achieving simultaneity in the presence of faults", *Proc. of the 26th IEEE Symp. on Foundation of Computer Science*, 1985, pp. 383–395.

[17] Chor, B. and R.L. Rivest, "A knapsack type public key cryptosystem based on arithmetic in finite fields" *Advances in Cryptology: Proceedings of Crypto84*, G.R. Blakely and D. Chaum. eds., Springer–Verlag, 1985, pp. 54–65.

[18] Coppersmith, D., "Fast Evaluation of Logarithms in Fields of Characteristic Two", *IEEE Trans. Inform. Theory*, vol. IT-30, pp. 587–594, 1984.

[19] Cover, T.M., "Enumerative Source Encoding", *IEEE Trans. Inform. Theory*, vol IT-19, pp. 73–77, 1973.

[20] Diffie, W. and M. Hellman, "New directions in cryptography", *IEEE Trans. Inform. Theory*, vol. IT-22, pp. 644–654, 1976.

[21] Feller, W., *An Introduction to Probability Theory and its Applications*, John Wiley and Sons, Vol. I, 1962.

[22] Garey, M. and D. Johnson, *Computers and intractability*, W. H. Freeman and Company, New York, 1979.

[23] Goldreich, O., "On the Number of Close-and-Equal Pairs of Bits in a String (with Implications on the Security of RSA's L.s.b.)", *Advances in Cryptology: Proceedings of EuroCrypt84*, T. Beth et al., eds., Springer–Verlag, 1985, pp. 127–141. (Also available as Technical memo TM-256, Laboratory for Computer Science, MIT, March 1984.)

[24] Goldwasser, S., "Probabilistic Encryption: Theory and Applications", Ph.D. dissertation, University of California at Berkeley, 1984.

[25] Goldwasser, S. and S. Micali, "Probabilistic Encryption", *Jour. of Computer and System Science*, Vol. 28, No. 2, 1984, pp. 270-299.

[26] Goldwasser, S., S. Micali, and P. Tong, "Why and How to Establish a Private Code on a Public Network", *Proc. of the 23rd IEEE Symp. on Foundation of Computer Science*, 1982, pp. 134-144.

[27] Halberstram, H. and K.F. Roth, *Sequences*, Springer-Verlag, New York, 1983.

[28] Kannan, R., "Improved algorithms for integer programming and related lattice problems", *Proceedings of the Fifteenth Annual Symposium on Theory of Computing*, ACM, pp. 193–206, 1983.

[29] Knuth, D.E. *The art of computer programming*, Vol. 2, *Seminumerical algorithms*, second edition, Addison-Wesley, Reading, 1981.

[30] Knuth, D.E. and L.T. Pardo, "Analysis of a simple factorization algorithm", *Theoretical Computer Science* 3 (no. 3), 1976, pp. 321–348.

[31] Lagarias, J.C. and A.M. Odlyzko, "Solving low-density subset sum problems", *Jour. of the ACM*, Vol. 32 no. 1, January 1985, pp. 229–246.

[32] Lenstra A.K., H.W. Lenstra Jr., and L. Lovasz, "Factoring polynomials with rational coefficients", *Math. Ann.* 261, pp. 515–534, 1982.

[33]   Long, D.L. and A. Wigderson, "How Discreet is Discrete Log ?", *15th ACM Symp. on theory of Computation*, April 1983, pp. 413-420.

[34]   McEliece, R.J., "A public-key cryptosystem based on algebraic coding theory", *DSN Progress Report 42-44*, pp. 114–116, 1978.

[35]   Merkle, R.C. and M. Hellman, "Hiding information and signatures in trap-door knapsacks", *IEEE Trans. Inform. Theory*, vol. IT-24, pp. 525–530, 1978.

[36]   Niven I. and H.S. Zuckerman, *An introduction to the theory of numbers*, third edition, John Wiley and Sons, New York, 1972.

[37]   Odlyzko, M.O., "Cryptanalytic attacks on the multiplicative knapsack cryptosystem and on Shamir's fast signature scheme", preprint, 1983.

[38]   Pohlig, R.C. and M. Hellman, "An improved algorithm for computing logarithms over $GF(p)$ and its cryptographic significance", *IEEE Trans. Inform. Theory*, vol. IT-24, pp. 106–110, 1978.

[39]   Rabin, M.O., "Digitalized signatures and public-key functions as intractable as factorization", Technical report TR-212, Laboratory for Computer Science, MIT, 1979.

[40]   Rabin, M.O., "Probabilistic Algorithms in Finite Fields" *SIAM J. Comput.*, vol. 9, No. 2, pp. 273–280, 1980.

[41]   Renyi, A., *Probability theory*, North-Holland, 1970.

[42]   Rivest, R.L., A. Shamir, and L. Adelman, "On digital signatures and public key cryptosystems", *Commun. ACM*, vol. 21, pp. 120–126, 1978.

[43]   Schnorr, C.P. and W. Alexi, "RSA bits are $0.5+\varepsilon$ secure", *Advances in Cryptology: Proceedings of EuroCrypt84*, T. Beth et al., eds., Springer-Verlag, 1985, pp. 113–126.

[44]   Schroeppel, R. and A. Shamir, "A $T = O(2^{n/2})$, $S = O(2^{n/4})$ algorithm for certain NP-complete problems", *SIAM J. Comput.*, vol. 10, No. 3, pp. 456–464, 1981.

[45] Shamir, A., "A polynomial time algorithm for breaking the basic Merkle–Hellman cryptosystem", *Proceedings of the Twenty-Third Annual Symposium on Foundations of Computer Science*, IEEE, pp. 145–152, 1982.

[46] Shamir, A., "Embedding cryptographic trapdoors in arbitrary knapsack systems", Technical memo TM–230, Laboratory for Computer Science, MIT, September 1982.

[47] Shannon, C.E., "Communication theory of secrecy systems", *Bell System Tech. J.* 28, 1949, pp. 656–715.

[47] Vazirani,U.V. and V.V. Vazirani, "RSA Bits are $.732 + \epsilon$ Secure", *Advances in Cryptology: Proceedings of Crypto83*, Chaum,D. ed., Plenum Press, 1984, pp. 369-375.

[48] Vazirani,U.V. and V.V. Vazirani, "Efficient and Secure Pseudo Random Number Generation", *Proc. of the 25th IEEE Symp. on Foundation of Computer Science*, 1984, pp. 458-463.

[49] Williams, H.C., "A Modification of the RSA Public-Key Encryption Procedure", *IEEE Trans. Inform. Theory*, vol. IT-26, 1980, pp. 726–729.

[50] Yao, A.C., "Theory and Applications of Trapdoor Functions", *Proc. of the 23rd IEEE Symp. on Foundation of Computer Science*, 1982, pp. 80-91.

Index

approximate magnitude 28,36
basis reduction algorithm 59,64
binary search 14
bit security 10,32
Bose-Chowla theorem 45
brute force attack 61
Chernoff bound 24,27
Chebyshev inequality 31
discrete logarithm 39,52,63
density of knapsack 58,64
Euclidean norm 59,65
error doubling 26
exponentiation 8,39,50
exclusive-or thechnique 40
factoring 2,35
finite field 45,52,57
gcd of integers 20
gcd of polynomials 56
indistinguishability 33,39
information rate 41,50
irreducible polynomial 48
Jacobi symbol 3,35
knapsack problem 44
knapsack-type systems 4,43
lattice 55,64

least-significant bit 4,16,32
Legendre symbol 35
low density attack 43,58,64
multiplicative properties 8
multiplicative generator 46,48
mutual independence 24,27
NP complete 44
oracle 3,10,23,32,36
parity bit 12
pairwise independence 28,31
partial factorization 38
prime factors 48,52
probabilistic encryption 2,40
pseudo-random generators 39
quadratic residuosity 2,40
Rabin's encryption 35
Rabin's encryption, modified 36
relatively prime integers 22
RSA encryption 8
RSA reducible 11
superincreasing sequence 43
simultaneous security 33,39
special vector 58,64
successive squaring 8,53
two-points based sampling 28
unpredictability 33,39

wraparound	16
zero-one knapsack	65

$[\cdot]_N$	8
$\left(\frac{\cdot}{N}\right)$ (Jacobi symbol)	35
$abs_N(\cdot)$	12
$d(A)$ (knapsack density)	58
d_α (critical density)	65
dx-measurement	17,23
$E(\cdot)$ (knapsack)	45
$E_N(\cdot)$ (RSA)	8
$E_N(\cdot)$ (Rabin)	36
$\varepsilon(n)$-oracle	10
$\varepsilon(n)$-secure	10
$half_N(\cdot)$	13
$GF(p)$	45
$L_N(\cdot)$	12
M_N	35
$\mathcal{O}_\mathcal{H}$	13
$\mathcal{O}_\mathcal{L}$	13
$par_N(\cdot)$	12
π (scrambling permutation)	48
$\varphi(N)$	8
R (information rate)	50
S_N	35
Z_N	7
Z_N^*	8

The MIT Press, with Peter Denning as consulting editor, publishes computer science books in the following series:

ACM Doctoral Dissertation Award and Distinguished Dissertation Series

Artificial Intelligence, Patrick Winston and Michael Brady, editors

Charles Babbage Institute Reprint Series for the History of Computing, Martin Campbell-Kelly, editor

Computer Systems, Herb Schwetman, editor

Foundations of Computing, Michael Garey, editor

History of Computing, I. Bernard Cohen and William Aspray, editors

Information Systems, Michael Lesk, editor

Logic Programming, Ehud Shapiro, editor

The MIT Electrical Engineering and Computer Science Series

Scientific Computation, Dennis Gannon, editor